The Australian Women's Weekly
Weekly
cookbooks

Whenever I think fast food these days, I usually think Asian and, more specifically, my local Thai takeaway. But this can get a bit expensive and quite honestly, with this lovely new collection of recipes, it's just as easy to whip up my own version of our favourite pad thai as it is to order it. And it's infinitely fresher and cheaper. There's sure to be a recipe here that will become *your* family's favourite fast food – all of them are so quick and delicious, the major difficulty will be deciding which one.

Pamela Clark

Food Editor

contents

asian ingredients

bamboo shoots the shoots of bamboo plants, available in cans.

basil, thai also known as bai kaprow or holy basil; has smaller, crinkly leaves with a strong, somewhat-bitter flavour, and is most often used in stir-fries.

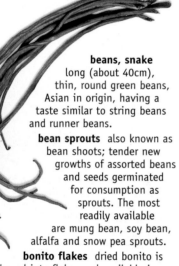

beans, snake long (about 40cm), thin, round green beans, Asian in origin, having a taste similar to string beans and runner beans.

bean sprouts also known as bean shoots; tender new growths of assorted beans and seeds germinated for consumption as sprouts. The most readily available are mung bean, soy bean, alfalfa and snow pea sprouts.

bonito flakes dried bonito is shaved into flakes and available in cellophane packs; larger, coarser flakes are used to make dashi while the finer shavings are used as a garnish. Keep in an airtight container after opening.

breadcrumbs, japanese also known as panko. Larger pieces than western-type breadcrumbs.

cardamom native to India and used extensively in its cuisine; can be purchased in pod, seed or ground form. Has a distinctive aromatic, sweetly rich flavour and is one of the world's most expensive spices.

chilli

FLAKES crushed dried chillies.

POWDER the Asian variety is the hottest, made from ground chillies; it can be used as a substitute for fresh chillies in the proportion of 1/2 teaspoon ground chilli powder to 1 medium chopped fresh chilli.

SAUCE we use a hot Chinese variety made of chillies, salt and vinegar; use sparingly, increasing amounts to taste. Sweet chilli sauce is a comparatively mild, Thai sauce made from red chillies, sugar, garlic and vinegar.

THAI bright-red to dark-green in colour, they are small, hot chillies.

chinese barbecued duck traditionally cooked in special ovens, this duck has a sweet-sticky coating made from soy sauce, sherry, five-spice and hoisin sauce; available from Asian food stores.

chinese barbecued pork also known as char siew. Traditionally cooked in special ovens, this pork has a sweet-sticky coating made from soy sauce, sherry, five-spice and hoisin sauce. It is available from Asian food stores.

chinese green vegetables these vegetables have different names from one region to the next; we have listed many alternative names for each vegetable.

BOK CHOY also known as bak choy, pak choi, chinese white cabbage and chinese chard; fresh, mild mustard taste. Baby bok choy is smaller and more tender than bok choy.

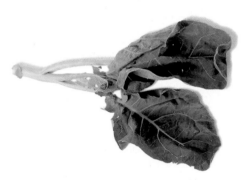

CHINESE BROCCOLI also known as gai lum, gai larn and chinese kale; it is traditionally served with oyster sauce. Prized more for its stems than coarse leaves, it is served steamed, stir-fried and in soups and noodle dishes.

CHINESE CABBAGE also known as peking cabbage, wong bok or petsai; the pale-green, crinkly leaves of this elongated cabbage only require brief cooking. Also the cabbage which forms the basis of the pickled Korean condiment, kim chi.

CHOY SUM also known as flowering bok choy, flowering-white or chinese-white cabbage; the stems, leaves and yellow flowers are served steamed, stir-fried and in soups.

chives, garlic also known as chinese chives; have flat leaves and stronger flavour than chives.

cinnamon stick dried inner bark of the shoots of the cinnamon tree.

cloves dried flower buds of a tropical tree; used whole or in ground form.

coconut

CREAM the first pressing from grated mature coconut flesh; available in cans and cartons.

DESICCATED unsweetened, concentrated, dried shredded coconut.

MILK the second pressing (less rich) from grated mature coconut flesh; available in cans and cartons. A lower-fat type is also available.

SHREDDED thin strips of dried coconut.

coriander also known as cilantro or chinese parsley; bright-green leafy herb with a pungent flavour. Often stirred into a dish just before serving for maximum impact.

curry

GREEN PASTE commercial versions consist of red onion, green chilli, soy bean oil, garlic, galangal, lemon grass, shrimp paste, citrus peel and coriander seeds.

LEAVES available fresh or dried and have a mild curry flavour; use like bay leaves.

PASTE some recipes in this book call for commercially prepared pastes of various strength and flavours, ranging from the mild tikka and medium madras to the fiery vindaloo. Use whichever one you feel suits your spice-level tolerance best.

RED PASTE commercial versions consist of chilli, onion, garlic, oil, lemon rind, shrimp paste, cumin, paprika, turmeric and pepper.

TANDOORI PASTE commercial versions consist of garlic, tamarind, ginger, coriander, chilli and spices.

TIKKA PASTE commercial versions consist of chilli, coriander, cumin, lentil flour, garlic, ginger, oil, turmeric, cinnamon, fennel, pepper, cloves and cardamom.

VINDALOO PASTE a fiery hot/sour flavour consisting of coriander, cumin, turmeric, chilli, ginger, garlic, tamarind, lentil flour and spices.

POWDER a blend of ground spices used for convenience when making Indian food. Can consist of some of the following spices in varying proportions: dried chilli, cinnamon, coriander, cumin, fennel, fenugreek, mace, cardamom and turmeric. Choose mild or hot to suit your taste and the recipe.

dashi the basic fish and seaweed stock that accounts for the distinctive flavour of many Japanese dishes; made from dried bonito flakes and kelp (konbu). Instant dashi powder, also known as dashi-no-moto, is a concentrated granulated powder. Dashi is available from Asian specialty stores.

eggplant, thai pea a little larger than a green pea and of a similar shape; the colour ranges from white streaked with green through to shades of purple.

fish sauce also called nam pla or nuoc nam; made from pulverised salted fermented fish. Has a pungent smell and strong taste; use sparingly.

five-spice powder a fragrant mixture of ground cinnamon, cloves, star anise, sichuan pepper and fennel seeds.

galangal also known as laos; a dried root that is a member of the ginger family, used whole or ground, having a piquant peppery flavour.

garam masala a blend of spices, originating in North India; based on varying proportions of fennel, cloves, cardamom, cinnamon, coriander, and cumin, roasted and ground together.

ghee clarified butter; with the milk solids removed, this fat can be heated to a high temperature without burning.

ginger

FRESH also known as green or root ginger; the thick gnarled root of a tropical plant. Can be kept, peeled, covered with dry sherry in a jar and refrigerated, or frozen in an airtight container.

PICKLED originating from Japan and available, packaged, from Asian food stores; thin, light pink shavings of ginger pickled in a mixture of vinegar, sugar and natural colouring.

hoisin sauce a thick, sweet and spicy chinese paste made from salted fermented soy beans, onions and garlic; used as a marinade or baste, or to accent stir-fries and barbecued or roasted foods.

kaffir lime leaves aromatic leaves of a small citrus tree bearing a wrinkle-skinned yellow-green fruit originally grown in South Africa and South-East Asia.

kecap manis Indonesian thick soy sauce which has sugar and spices added.

lemon grass a tall, clumping, lemon-smelling and -tasting, sharp-edged grass; the white lower part of the stem is used, finely chopped, in cooking.

mirin a sweet low-alcohol rice wine used in Japanese cooking; sometimes referred to simply as rice wine but should not be confused with sake, the Japanese rice wine made for drinking.

mushrooms

DRIED SHIITAKE also known as donko or dried chinese mushrooms; have a unique meaty flavour. Sold dried; soak to rehydrate before use.

OYSTER also known as abalone mushrooms; grey-white mushroom shaped like a fan.

SHIITAKE also called chinese black mushrooms.

mustard, japanese available from Asian grocery stores in a tube of ready-to-use paste, or powder form.

noodles

BEAN THREAD VERMICELLI also known as bean thread noodles, or cellophane or glass noodles; can be soaked in warm water or deep-fried.

FLAT RICE fresh soft white noodles.

FRESH EGG made from wheat flour and eggs; varying in thickness from fine strands to pieces as thick as a shoelace.

FRIED crispy egg noodles packaged (commonly a 100g packet) already deep-fried.

HOKKIEN also known as stir-fry noodles; fresh wheat flour noodles resembling thick, yellow-brown spaghetti needing no pre-cooking before use.

RAMEN a crinkly or straight dried wheat noodle, sold in cakes.

RICE STICK a dried noodle, available flat and wide or very thin; made from rice flour and water.

SOBA thin spaghetti-like pale-brown noodle made from varying amounts of buckwheat and plain flour; used in soups or eaten cold with dashi and chopped.

UDON available fresh and dried, these Japanese broad white wheat noodles are similar to the ones in homemade chicken noodle soup.

nori sheets of paper-thin dried black seaweed used in Japanese cooking as a flavouring, garnish or for sushi.

oil

PEANUT pressed from ground peanuts; most commonly used oil in Asian cooking because of its high smoke point.

SESAME made from roasted, crushed, white sesame seeds; a flavouring rather than a cooking medium.

plum sauce a thick, sweet and sour dipping sauce made from plums, vinegar, sugar, chillies and spices.

rice paper also known as banh trang. Made from rice paste and stamped into rounds. Stores well at room temperature, although they are quite brittle and will break if dropped. Dipped momentarily in water they become pliable wrappers for fried food and for eating fresh (uncooked) vegetables.

rice wine a sweet, gold-coloured, low-alcohol wine made from fermented rice.

sake Japan's favourite rice wine, sake is used in cooking, marinating and as part of dipping sauces. If sake is unavailable, dry sherry, vermouth or brandy can be substituted. When consumed as a drink, it is served warm; to do this, stand the container in hot water for about 20 minutes to warm the sake.

sambal oelek (also ulek or olek) Indonesian in origin; a salty paste made from ground chillies and vinegar.

seeds

BLACK MUSTARD also known as brown mustard seeds; more pungent than the white (or yellow) seeds used in most prepared mustards.

SESAME black and white are the most common of the oval seeds, however, there are red and brown varieties also. To toast: spread seeds evenly on oven tray, toast in moderate oven briefly.

YELLOW MUSTARD also known as white mustard seeds.

shrimp paste also known as trasi and blanchan; a strong-scented, almost solid preserved paste made of salted dried shrimp. Used as a pungent flavouring in many South-East Asian soups and sauces.

sichuan pepper also known as szechuan or chinese pepper; small, red-brown aromatic seeds resembling black peppercorns, they have a peppery-lemon flavour.

soy sauce made from fermented soy beans. Several variations are available in most supermarkets and Asian food stores.

DARK used for colour as well as flavour, particularly in North Chinese cooking.

LIGHT as the name suggests, light in colour. We used a light soy sauce of Japanese origin. While light in colour, it is generally quite salty.

SALT-REDUCED we used a sauce with 46% of the salt removed after it is made.

star anise a dried star-shaped pod that imparts an astringent aniseed flavour.

sugar, palm very fine sugar from the coconut palm. It is sold in cakes, also known as gula jawa, gula melaka and jaggery. Brown or black sugar can be substituted.

sukiyaki sauce bottled sauce of Japanese origin, a blend of soy sauce, mirin, sugar and salt; used as a flavouring.

tamarind concentrate a thick, purple-black, ready-to-use paste extracted from the pulp of the tamarind bean; used as is, with no soaking, stirred into sauces and casseroles.

tofu also known as bean curd, an off-white, custard-like product made from the "milk" of crushed soy beans; comes fresh as soft or firm, and processed as fried or pressed dried sheets. Leftover fresh tofu can be refrigerated in water (changed daily) for up to four days. Silken tofu refers to the method by which it is made, where it is strained through silk.

BEAN CURD POUCHES pockets of bean curd (tofu) which are able to be opened out to take a filling. Available from Asian food stores.

FRIED packaged fried bean curd consists of cubes of soft bean curd, deep-fried until the surface is brown and crusty and the inside almost dry.

FIRM made by compressing bean curd to remove most of the water. Used in a variety of dishes.

SOFT mainly used in soups.

vietnamese mint not a mint at all, this narrow-leafed, pungent herb, also known as cambodian mint and laksa leaf, is widely used in South-East Asian soups and salads.

vinegar

RICE made from fermented rice, colourless and flavoured with sugar and salt; also known as seasoned rice vinegar.

RICE WINE made from rice wine lees (sediment), salt and alcohol.

wasabi green Asian horseradish used to make a fiery sauce traditionally served with Japanese raw fish dishes.

wonton wrappers gow gee, egg or spring roll pastry sheets can be substituted.

soups

combination wonton soup

PREPARATION TIME 30 MINUTES • COOKING TIME 10 MINUTES

This soup is a favourite in southern China, where it originated, and has a firm following worldwide thanks to its inclusion on the menu of many Chinese restaurants in the West.

150g chicken mince
1 green onion, sliced thinly
2 tablespoons light soy sauce
16 wonton wrappers
24 medium uncooked
    prawns (600g)
1.5 litres (6 cups) chicken stock
100g Chinese barbecued pork,
    sliced thinly
100g fresh shiitake mushrooms,
    sliced thinly
150g baby bok choy,
    chopped coarsely
4 green onions, sliced thinly, extra

1 Combine chicken, onion and half of the sauce in small bowl.

2 Place heaped teaspoons of chicken mixture in centre of each wonton wrapper; brush edges with a little water, pinch edges together to seal.

3 Shell and devein prawns.

4 Bring stock to a boil in large saucepan, add wontons; cook, uncovered, about 3 minutes or until wontons are just cooked through.

5 Add prawns, remaining sauce, pork and mushrooms; cook, uncovered, until prawns just change colour. Add bok choy and extra onion; cook, uncovered, until bok choy just wilts.

SERVES 4

per serving 9.1g fat; 1155kJ

tip Uncooked wontons are suitable to freeze for up to three months. You don't have to defrost them; just remove from freezer and simmer in stock until cooked through.

serving suggestion Serve spring rolls as a starter before this soup.

tom yum goong

PREPARATION TIME 10 MINUTES • COOKING TIME 15 MINUTES

Thailand's legendary hot and sour prawn soup is not for the faint-hearted, thanks to a good dose of chilli and lots of lime juice and lemon grass. The tangy flavour is a crucial element to this dish, but you can omit the chillies if you can't stand the heat. You will need a piece of ginger about 1.5cm long for this recipe.

20 medium uncooked
    prawns (500g)
1 litre (4 cups) chicken stock
1 litre (4 cups) water
2 tablespoons coarsely
    chopped lemon grass
8 kaffir lime leaves
15g fresh ginger, sliced thinly
2 red thai chillies, seeded,
    chopped finely
1/4 cup (60ml) lime juice
1 tablespoon fish sauce
1/4 cup loosely packed fresh
    coriander leaves
2 green onions, sliced thinly

1 Shell and devein prawns, leaving tails intact.

2 Heat combined stock, water, lemon grass, lime leaves, ginger and chilli in large saucepan; bring to a boil. Reduce heat; simmer, uncovered, 10 minutes. Strain mixture through muslin-lined strainer into large saucepan; discard solids.

3 Add juice and sauce to stock mixture; bring to a boil. Add prawns; cook, uncovered, until prawns just change colour. Stir in remaining ingredients just before serving.

SERVES 4

per serving 1.5g fat; 382kJ

tip The stock mixture can be made a day ahead; store, covered, in the refrigerator until just before serving time.

serving suggestion Serve this soup as a starter before pad thai (page 32).

beef with ramen and mushrooms

PREPARATION TIME 10 MINUTES (plus standing time) • COOKING TIME 20 MINUTES

Ramen is a kind of instant wheat noodle, available in both crinkly or straight forms. The most popular Japanese fast food, these noodles are available from Asian grocery stores and some supermarkets.

8 dried shiitake mushrooms
2 tablespoons peanut oil
500g beef strips
4 green onions, sliced thinly
2 cloves garlic, crushed
2 teaspoons grated fresh ginger
1 litre (4 cups) beef stock
3 cups (750ml) water
1 tablespoon light soy sauce
2 tablespoons rice wine
180g ramen

1 Place mushrooms in small heatproof bowl, cover with boiling water; stand 20 minutes, drain. Discard stems; slice caps thinly.

2 Heat half of the oil in large saucepan; cook beef, in batches, until browned all over.

3 Heat remaining oil in same pan; cook half of the onion with garlic and ginger, stirring, until onion softens. Add stock, the water, sauce and wine; bring to a boil.

4 Add mushrooms, beef and noodles; bring to a boil. Reduce heat; simmer, uncovered, about 5 minutes or until noodles are tender. Serve soup sprinkled with remaining onion.

SERVES 4

per serving 15.8g fat; 1805kJ

tip Beef strips can be cut from varying cuts of lean beef, ranging from round, blade and topside steak to rump, eye and rib-eye (scotch) fillet.

serving suggestion For a flavour boost, serve this dish with finely chopped chilli on the side.

laksa lemak

PREPARATION TIME 10 MINUTES • COOKING TIME 10 MINUTES

*There are countless versions of this Malaysian spicy noodle soup, each one delicious.
Our recipe features a variety of vegetables but, if you wish, you can add other
ingredients such as prawns or chicken. We used the dried rice noodles also known
as rice stick noodles, which are about 5mm wide, in this recipe.*

**1 litre (4 cups) chicken stock
1 cup (250ml) water
1/3 cup (80ml) chilli garlic sauce
1/3 cup (80ml) fish sauce
1/4 cup (60ml) oyster sauce
1 tablespoon curry powder
400ml coconut cream
250g dried rice noodles
300g baby bok choy, trimmed
100g snow peas, halved
200g fresh baby corn, halved
150g fried tofu, chopped coarsely
3 cups (240g) bean sprouts**

1   Combine stock, the water, sauces, curry powder and coconut
    cream in large saucepan; bring to a boil. Reduce heat; simmer,
    uncovered, 10 minutes.

2   Meanwhile, place noodles in large heatproof bowl, cover with boiling
    water, stand until just tender; drain.

3   Add bok choy, snow peas, corn and tofu to stock mixture; cook,
    uncovered, until vegetables are just tender.

4   Divide noodles among serving bowls, ladle soup into each bowl
    and top with sprouts.

SERVES 4

per serving 25.8g fat; 2432kJ

tip You can buy fried tofu from Asian supermarkets or you can cut fresh
tofu into cubes and shallow-fry it in vegetable oil until browned lightly.

serving suggestion Serve this soup after a starter of gado gado (page 38).

thai sweet and sour soup

PREPARATION TIME 10 MINUTES • COOKING TIME 15 MINUTES

Many Thai soups are hot and sour, but this one offers a pleasant change to the palate, balancing the traditional sour flavour with a refreshing sweetness.

1 litre (4 cups) chicken stock
1¹/₂ cups (375ml) water
1 tablespoon coarsely chopped
    lemon grass
1 red thai chilli, halved
1 lime, halved
1 small brown onion (80g), halved
340g chicken breast fillets,
    sliced thinly
3 trimmed sticks celery (225g),
    sliced thinly
2 medium carrots (240g),
    sliced thinly
1 small leek (200g), sliced thinly
450g can pineapple pieces
    in natural juice
2 tablespoons lime juice
2 green onions, sliced thinly

1 Combine stock, the water, lemon grass, chilli, lime and brown onion in large saucepan; bring to a boil. Reduce heat; simmer, uncovered, 5 minutes. Strain stock mixture through muslin-lined strainer into large saucepan; discard solids.

2 Add chicken, celery, carrot and leek to stock mixture; bring to a boil. Reduce heat; simmer, uncovered, about 5 minutes or until chicken is cooked through.

3 Meanwhile, strain pineapple over small bowl; reserve pineapple and two tablespoons of the juice.

4 Remove stock mixture from heat; stir in pineapple, reserved juice and lime juice. Serve soup topped with green onion.

SERVES 4

per serving 6g fat; 922kJ

tip Soup can be made a day ahead; store, covered, in the refrigerator.
serving suggestion In a Thai meal, soups like this are served with other dishes – such as meat or fish curries and boiled rice – and are either sipped during the meal or spooned over rice.

transparent noodle soup

PREPARATION TIME 10 MINUTES • COOKING TIME 20 MINUTES

*Dried mung beans are ground into flour to make bean thread noodles. These very fine, almost
transparent noodles are also known as bean thread vermicelli, or cellophane or glass noodles.*

100g bean thread noodles
**1 red thai chilli, seeded,
    sliced thinly**
2 cloves garlic, crushed
**1¹/₂ tablespoons thinly sliced
    lemon grass**
2 teaspoons grated fresh ginger
2¹/₂ cups (625ml) chicken stock
3¹/₂ cups (875ml) water
**340g chicken breast fillets,
    sliced thinly**
**2 tablespoons finely chopped
    fresh mint**
**¹/₄ cup loosely packed
    fresh coriander**
2 teaspoons fish sauce
2 tablespoons light soy sauce

1 Place noodles in medium heatproof bowl, cover with boiling water,
  stand until just tender; drain.

2 Cook chilli, garlic, lemon grass and ginger in large non stick saucepan,
  stirring, until fragrant. Stir in stock and the water; bring to a boil.

3 Add chicken; return to a boil. Reduce heat; simmer, uncovered,
  skimming occasionally, about 5 minutes or until chicken is cooked
  through. Add noodles and remaining ingredients to soup; stir until hot.

SERVES 4

per serving 5.4g fat; 867kJ

tip Try using rice vermicelli in this recipe, but be sure to follow the
manufacturer's instructions regarding their preparation.

serving suggestion Serve this soup as part of a banquet consisting of
Thai beef salad (page 114), vegetable green curry (page 42) and
jasmine rice.

hot and sour soup

PREPARATION TIME 15 MINUTES • COOKING TIME 20 MINUTES

*We've adapted the northern Chinese original to create a hearty, mildly hot soup.
We used cracked black pepper in this recipe but you can crush and use authentic
Sichuan peppercorns if you have access to an Asian grocery store.*

1.25 litres (5 cups) chicken stock
3 cups (750ml) water
1 clove garlic, crushed
2 teaspoons grated fresh ginger
1 tablespoon sambal oelek
2 tablespoons light soy sauce
100g pork fillets, sliced thinly
100g chicken tenderloins, sliced thinly
8 fresh shiitake mushrooms, sliced thinly
$1/2$ cup (100g) drained canned bamboo shoots
2 tablespoons sake
$1/3$ cup (80ml) lime juice
1 teaspoon cracked black pepper
2 tablespoons cornflour
2 tablespoons water, extra
3 eggs, beaten lightly
300g soft tofu, chopped coarsely
4 green onions, sliced thinly

1 Combine stock and the water in large saucepan; bring to a boil.
   Stir in garlic, ginger, sambal and sauce; simmer, uncovered, about
   3 minutes or until fragrant.

2 Add pork, chicken, mushrooms, bamboo shoots, sake, juice and pepper;
   bring to a boil. Reduce heat; simmer, uncovered, about 5 minutes or
   until meat is cooked through.

3 Blend cornflour with the extra water; add to stock mixture.
   Cook, stirring, until mixture boils and thickens slightly.

4 Gradually add egg, in a thin stream, to simmering soup, stirring
   continuously. Divide tofu and onion among bowls; pour hot soup over.

SERVES 4

per serving 19.6g fat; 1491kJ

tips You can replace the sambal oelek with fresh red chillies, if you prefer.
If fresh shiitake mushrooms are unavailable, use button mushrooms or
reconstituted dried shiitake mushrooms.

serving suggestion Enjoy this soup with sang choy bow (page 104)
and Chinese-style fried rice (page 26).

chicken and corn soup

PREPARATION TIME 10 MINUTES • COOKING TIME 20 MINUTES

We have the Chinese to thank for this comforting and nourishing combination that has been embraced by the world.

2 teaspoons peanut oil
2 green onions, sliced finely
1 clove garlic, crushed
1 litre (4 cups) chicken stock
1 litre (4 cups) water
**170g chicken breast fillets,
  chopped finely**
310g can creamed corn
310g can corn kernels
1 tablespoon cornflour
1/4 cup (60ml) water, extra
1 egg, beaten lightly

1 Heat oil in large saucepan; cook onion and garlic, stirring constantly, until onion softens.

2 Add stock and the water to onion mixture; bring to a boil. Reduce heat, add chicken; simmer, uncovered, about 5 minutes or until chicken is cooked through.

3 Add both corns and cornflour blended with the extra water. Cook, stirring, until mixture boils and thickens slightly. Gradually add egg, in a thin stream, to simmering soup.

SERVES 4

per serving 8.1g fat; 1138kJ

tip You can make your own chicken stock (see page 118), or you can use one of the commercially prepared versions available in supermarkets.

serving suggestion Serve with your favourite Chinese main, such as Mongolian garlic lamb (page 88), plain rice and stir-fried Asian vegetables.

beef noodle soup

PREPARATION TIME 10 MINUTES • COOKING TIME 35 MINUTES

Star anise is the main ingredient of five-spice powder and is also used to enhance soups, stews and teas throughout Asia, either whole or in pieces. You can buy it from Asian grocery stores and some supermarkets. You will need a piece of ginger about 5cm long for this recipe.

600g fresh rice noodles
1 litre (4 cups) beef stock
2 cups (500ml) water
1 medium brown onion (150g),
    chopped coarsely
2 star anise
50g fresh ginger, peeled,
    chopped coarsely
1/2 teaspoon black peppercorns
1 teaspoon cardamom pods
1 cinnamon stick
650g beef rump steak,
    sliced thinly
1¹/2 cups (120g) bean sprouts
2 tablespoons finely shredded
    fresh mint
2 tablespoons finely shredded
    fresh coriander
2 red thai chillies, sliced thinly
3 green onions, sliced thinly

1 Rinse noodles under hot water; drain. Transfer to large bowl; separate noodles with fork.

2 Combine stock, the water, brown onion, star anise, ginger, peppercorns, cardamom and cinnamon in large saucepan; bring to a boil. Reduce heat; simmer, uncovered, 15 minutes. Strain stock mixture through muslin-lined strainer into large saucepan; discard solids.

3 Add beef to stock mixture; bring to a boil. Reduce heat; simmer, uncovered, until beef is cooked as desired. Divide noodles among serving bowls; top with stock mixture, sprouts, mint, coriander, chilli and green onion.

SERVES 4

per serving 9.2g fat; 2196kJ

tip Stock mixture can be made a day ahead; store, covered, in the refrigerator.

serving suggestion For added piquancy, serve with lemon or lime wedges.

thai pumpkin and prawn soup

PREPARATION TIME 15 MINUTES • COOKING TIME 15 MINUTES

In this Thai favourite, pumpkin and prawns are simmered in creamy coconut-flavoured stock, with herbs and spices adding a rich flavour.

24 medium uncooked
    prawns (600g)
1 tablespoon vegetable oil
1 medium brown onion (150g),
    sliced thinly
2 tablespoons thai green
    curry paste
2 cloves garlic, crushed
2 teaspoons grated fresh ginger
1 red thai chilli, seeded,
    chopped finely
1 tablespoon finely chopped
    lemon grass
3 cups (750ml) chicken stock
400ml light coconut milk
600g butternut pumpkin,
    sliced thinly

1 Shell and devein prawns, leaving tails intact.

2 Heat oil in large saucepan; cook onion, paste, garlic, ginger, chilli and lemon grass, stirring, until onion softens. Add stock and coconut milk; bring to a boil. Reduce heat, add pumpkin; cook, uncovered, until pumpkin is almost tender.

3 Add prawns; cook, uncovered, until prawns have just changed colour.

SERVES 4

per serving 16.1g fat; 1283kJ

tip This soup base (to the end of step 2) can be made a day ahead; store, covered, in the refrigerator. Just before serving, add prawns and cook until prawns change colour and soup is hot.

serving suggestion This dish makes a light meal on its own or can be served as part of a Thai banquet.

udon soup

PREPARATION TIME 10 MINUTES • COOKING TIME 10 MINUTES

Dashi is the basic bonito seaweed stock that accounts for the distinctive flavour of many Japanese dishes. Instant dashi powder, also known as dashi-no-moto, is a concentrated granulated powder that is available from Asian grocery stores and some supermarkets.

400g fresh udon
1.5 litres (6 cups) water
1½ teaspoons instant dashi
400g chicken breast fillets,
    sliced thinly
100g oyster mushrooms, halved
300g baby bok choy,
    chopped coarsely
1 cup (80g) bean sprouts
1 tablespoon light soy sauce
2 green onions, sliced thinly

1 Rinse noodles under hot water; drain. Transfer to large bowl; separate noodles with fork.

2 Combine the water and dashi in large saucepan; bring to a boil. Add chicken; simmer, uncovered, until chicken is cooked through.

3 Add noodles, mushrooms, bok choy, sprouts and sauce; bring to a boil. Reduce heat; simmer, uncovered, until bok choy just wilts. Sprinkle with onion to serve.

SERVES 4

per serving 6.7g fat; 1284kJ

tip Udon noodles are available either fresh or dried; these broad Japanese wheat noodles are similar to the ones in homemade chicken noodle soup. You can substitute your favourite noodles, but be sure to check the manufacturer's instructions regarding their preparation.

serving suggestion Stay with the Japanese accent by following this soup with stir-fried sukiyaki (page 102).

noodles and rice

fried noodles, chicken and bok choy

PREPARATION TIME 10 MINUTES • COOKING TIME 20 MINUTES

This recipe uses baby bok choy, but you can use the larger bok choy, also known as pak choi or chinese white cabbage, if you trim and slice it finely. This Asian green has a slightly-mustard taste, and both leaves and stems are used in stir-fries and soups.

250g dried thin rice noodles
1 tablespoon peanut oil
3 eggs, beaten lightly
1 medium brown onion (150g),
   chopped finely
2 cloves garlic, crushed
2 teaspoons grated fresh ginger
500g chicken mince
500g baby bok choy,
   chopped coarsely
1/4 cup (60ml) light soy sauce
1/2 cup loosely packed, coarsely
   chopped fresh coriander
3 cups (240g) bean sprouts

1 Place noodles in large heatproof bowl; cover with boiling water. Stand until just tender; drain.

2 Brush heated wok or large frying pan with a little of the oil. Add half of the egg; swirl to cover base of wok. Cook, covered, about 3 minutes or until cooked through. Remove omelette from wok; repeat with remaining egg. Roll omelettes tightly; slice thinly.

3 Heat remaining oil in wok; stir-fry onion, garlic and ginger until onion softens. Add chicken; stir-fry until chicken is cooked through.

4 Add bok choy, sauce and coriander; stir-fry until bok choy is just tender. Stir in noodles and sprouts; serve immediately, topped with omelette.

SERVES 4

per serving 19.8g fat; 2149kJ

tips Create a vegetarian version of this dish by substituting fried tofu for the chicken.

You can substitute choy sum or chinese broccoli for the bok choy.

serving suggestion Serve this dish as a main meal, after an appetiser of spring rolls or prawn toasts.

prawn noodle salad with mint, basil and coriander

PREPARATION TIME 30 MINUTES

Bean thread noodles, also known as bean thread vermicelli, or cellophane or glass noodles, are very fine, almost transparent noodles. They look similar to dried rice vermicelli but are tougher. Soak the noodles just long enough to soften them – any longer and they become soggy and start to break up.

200g bean thread noodles
18 medium cooked prawns (450g)
2 teaspoons fish sauce
1 tablespoon light soy sauce
2 tablespoons lime juice
1 tablespoon sugar
1 red thai chilli, chopped finely
1 lebanese cucumber (130g),
**   halved lengthways, seeded,**
**   sliced thinly**
250g cherry tomatoes, quartered
1/4 cup loosely packed, coarsely
**   chopped fresh mint**
1/4 cup loosely packed, coarsely
**   chopped fresh coriander**
1/4 cup loosely packed, coarsely
**   chopped fresh basil**

1 Place noodles in large heatproof bowl; cover with boiling water. Stand until just tender; drain. Rinse noodles under cold water; drain well. Chop noodles coarsely.

2 Shell and devein prawns; halve lengthways.

3 Combine sauces, juice, sugar and chilli in small bowl.

4 Combine noodles, prawns, sauce mixture, cucumber, tomato and herbs in large bowl; toss gently.

SERVES 4

per serving 1.5g fat; 1019kJ

tip For a milder version of this salad, remove and discard seeds from the chillies before chopping.

serving suggestion This dish makes a great accompaniment to Vietnamese omelette (page 48).

japanese fried noodles

PREPARATION TIME 10 MINUTES • COOKING TIME 15 MINUTES

Fried noodles are available in fast-food bars throughout Japan. The noodles, pre-cooked and drained, are tossed together with the vegetables and meat on a very hot barbecue plate before being served as an after-work snack to executives who eat them, standing up, at counters all over Tokyo.

250g dried wheat noodles
2 tablespoons peanut oil
500g pork fillets, sliced thinly
1 large brown onion (200g),
sliced thinly
1 medium red capsicum (200g),
sliced thinly
1 medium green capsicum (200g),
sliced thinly
2 cups (140g) coarsely shredded
chinese cabbage
1/4 cup (60ml) tonkatsu sauce
1/4 cup (60ml) sukiyaki sauce

1 Cook noodles in large saucepan of boiling water, uncovered, until just tender; drain. Rinse under cold water; drain well.

2 Meanwhile, heat half of the oil in wok or large frying pan; stir-fry pork, in batches, until browned all over.

3 Heat remaining oil in wok; stir-fry onion until soft. Add capsicums; stir-fry until just tender.

4 Return pork to wok with noodles, cabbage and sauces; stir-fry until cabbage just wilts.

SERVES 4

per serving 13.3g fat; 2068kJ

tip You can use soba, fresh hokkien or rice noodles in this dish.
serving suggestion Serve this dish with yakitori chicken (page 70).

chilli pork noodles

PREPARATION TIME 10 MINUTES • COOKING TIME 10 MINUTES

Udon, wide Japanese noodles made from wheat flour, are available fresh or dried from Asian supermarkets. You can substitute any dried flat wheat noodle, but check the manufacturer's instructions regarding their preparation.

500g udon
1 tablespoon peanut oil
2 tablespoons finely chopped
   garlic chives
3 cloves garlic, crushed
3 red thai chillies, seeded,
   chopped finely
500g pork mince
1/4 cup (60ml) light soy sauce
1/2 cup (125ml) chicken stock
1 cup (80g) bean sprouts
4 green onions, sliced thinly

1 Cook noodles in large saucepan of boiling water, uncovered, until just tender; drain.

2 Meanwhile, heat oil in wok or large frying pan; stir-fry chives, garlic and chilli until fragrant.

3 Add pork; stir-fry until cooked through. Add sauce and stock; stir-fry until hot.

4 Serve pork mixture on noodles; top with sprouts and onion.

SERVES 4

per serving 14.8g fat; 1789kJ

tip Dried udon are available in different thicknesses, so the cooking time will vary depending on the size.

serving suggestion Serve these delicious noodles with Asian greens in oyster sauce.

chinese-style fried rice

PREPARATION TIME 10 MINUTES • COOKING TIME 20 MINUTES

Chinese barbecued pork, also known as char siew, is traditionally cooked in special ovens and has a sweet-sticky coating made from soy sauce, sherry, five-spice and hoisin sauce; it is available from Asian barbecue takeaway stores. You will need to cook about 1 1/2 cups (300g) long-grain white rice for this recipe.

1 tablespoon peanut oil
3 eggs, beaten lightly
2 cloves garlic, crushed
2 teaspoons grated fresh ginger
6 green onions, sliced thinly
4 cups (600g) cold, cooked
   long-grain white rice
200g small shelled
   cooked prawns
200g Chinese barbecued pork,
   sliced thinly
1 cup (125g) frozen peas, thawed
1 cup (80g) bean sprouts
1/4 cup (60ml) light soy sauce

1 Brush wok or large frying pan with a little of the oil. Add half of the egg; swirl to cover base of wok. Cook, covered, about 3 minutes or until cooked through. Remove omelette from wok; repeat with remaining egg. Roll omelettes tightly; slice thinly.

2 Heat remaining oil in wok; stir-fry garlic, ginger and onion until fragrant. Add omelette, rice, prawns, pork, peas, sprouts and sauce; stir-fry until hot.

SERVES 4

per serving 16.9g fat; 2002kJ

tip You can substitute barbecued or grilled pork fillet for the Chinese barbecued pork.

serving suggestion Fried rice makes a delicious side dish for a variety of grilled and stir-fried meat and vegetarian main meals.

beef and rice noodles

PREPARATION TIME 15 MINUTES • COOKING TIME 20 MINUTES

This recipe uses chinese broccoli, which is also known as gai lum. Every part of chinese broccoli is edible and, while often used in stir-fries, it is also a popular side dish served on its own, fried in an oyster sauce.

500g fresh rice noodles
2 tablespoons peanut oil
500g beef fillets, sliced thinly
1 clove garlic, crushed
1 tablespoon grated fresh ginger
1 tablespoon finely chopped lemon grass
1 red thai chilli, seeded, chopped finely
1 tablespoon coarsely chopped fresh mint
1 large carrot (180g), halved lengthways, sliced thinly
200g fresh baby corn, halved lengthways
200g chinese broccoli, chopped coarsely
1 tablespoon brown sugar
2 teaspoons cornflour
1/4 cup (60ml) rice wine
1/4 cup (60ml) oyster sauce
2 tablespoons light soy sauce

1 Rinse noodles under hot water; drain. Transfer to large bowl; separate noodles with fork.

2 Heat half of the oil in wok or large frying pan; stir-fry beef, in batches, until browned all over.

3 Heat remaining oil in wok; stir-fry garlic, ginger, lemon grass, chilli and mint until fragrant. Add carrot and corn; stir-fry until carrot is just tender.

4 Return beef to wok with broccoli, sugar and blended cornflour, wine and sauces; stir-fry until broccoli just wilts, and sauce boils and thickens slightly. Add noodles; stir-fry until hot.

SERVES 4

per serving 16.5g fat; 2011kJ

tip Fresh rice noodles must be rinsed under hot water to remove starch and excess oil before using. You can substitute egg noodles for the rice noodles, if you prefer.

serving suggestion Serve this dish after an appetiser of prawn gow gees or other steamed dim sum.

mee goreng

PREPARATION TIME 15 MINUTES • COOKING TIME 15 MINUTES

Mee goreng, from Indonesia, translates simply as fried noodles. There are many different versions of this Asian mainstay — all of them easy to make. This recipe uses prawns, but it's often made with chicken, pork or beef.

500g fresh rice noodles
**20 medium uncooked
  prawns (500g)**
1 tablespoon peanut oil
3 eggs, beaten lightly
2 cloves garlic, crushed
2 teaspoons grated fresh ginger
**4 trimmed sticks celery (300g),
  sliced thinly**
4 green onions, sliced thinly
**1/4 cup loosely packed, coarsely
  chopped fresh coriander**
1/4 cup (60ml) light soy sauce
**1/2 cup (75g) roasted unsalted
  peanuts, chopped coarsely**
**1 lebanese cucumber (130g),
  halved lengthways, seeded,
  sliced thinly**

1 Rinse noodles under hot water; drain. Transfer to large bowl; separate noodles with fork. Shell and devein prawns; cut in half lengthways.

2 Brush heated wok or large frying pan with a little of the oil. Add half of the egg; swirl to cover base of wok. Cook, covered, about 3 minutes or until cooked through. Remove omelette from wok; repeat with remaining egg. Roll omelettes tightly; slice thinly.

3 Heat remaining oil in wok; stir-fry prawns, garlic, ginger and celery until prawns just change colour. Add noodles, onion, coriander and sauce; stir-fry until heated through. Serve immediately sprinkled with omelette, peanuts and cucumber.

SERVES 4

per serving 18.4g fat; 1678kJ

tip You can substitute your favourite noodles for the rice noodles. However, you may need to adjust the cooking time.

serving suggestion You could serve this dish with a small bowl of finely sliced red thai chilli or chilli sauce on the side, for those who like it hot.

special birthday noodles

PREPARATION TIME 15 MINUTES • COOKING TIME 15 MINUTES

In China, noodles are a symbol of longevity and, as such, are often served at birthday parties and weddings... or just about any other occasion actually! This recipe is topped with hard-boiled egg – a symbol of fertility.

500g fresh thick egg noodles
2 tablespoons peanut oil
600g beef fillets, sliced thinly
2 cloves garlic, crushed
1 teaspoon grated fresh ginger
2 red thai chillies, seeded,
** chopped finely**
1 tablespoon cornflour
1/4 cup (60ml) light soy sauce
1/4 cup (60ml) hoisin sauce
1/2 cup (125ml) water
2 tablespoons rice vinegar
4 green onions, sliced thinly
2 hard-boiled eggs, sliced thinly

1 Rinse noodles under hot water; drain. Transfer to large bowl; separate noodles with fork.

2 Heat oil in wok or large frying pan; stir-fry beef, in batches, until browned all over. Return beef to wok with garlic, ginger and chilli; stir-fry until fragrant.

3 Blend cornflour, sauces, the water and vinegar in small bowl; add mixture to wok. Stir-fry until sauce boils and thickens; toss in onion and noodles. Serve immediately, topped with egg slices.

SERVES 4

per serving 21.6g fat; 2886kJ

tip To make this a more substantial meal, add thinly sliced vegetables such as capsicum, zucchini and carrots.

serving suggestion Accompany this dish with prawn crackers.

pad thai

This traditional Thai noodle dish is delicious as an accompaniment or as a complete meal. Rice noodles come in varying thicknesses, from the very thin strands to the flat and wide versions. In Thailand, they usually use sen lek, a 5mm-wide rice noodle, sometimes called rice stick noodles.

12 medium cooked prawns (300g)
250g dried rice noodles
3 tablespoons finely chopped palm sugar
1 tablespoon lime juice
1 tablespoon light soy sauce
1 tablespoon tomato sauce
2 tablespoons mild chilli sauce
2 tablespoons fish sauce
2 teaspoons peanut oil
220g chicken mince
200g pork mince
1 clove garlic, crushed
1 tablespoon grated fresh ginger
3 eggs, beaten lightly
2 green onions, sliced thinly
1 cup (80g) bean sprouts
1/2 cup (75g) roasted unsalted peanuts, chopped coarsely
1/3 cup loosely packed, coarsely chopped fresh coriander

1 Shell and devein prawns, leaving tails intact.

2 Place noodles in large heatproof bowl; cover with boiling water. Stand until just tender; drain. Cover to keep warm.

3 Combine sugar, juice and sauces in small bowl.

4 Heat oil in wok or large frying pan; stir-fry chicken, pork, garlic and ginger until meat is cooked through. Add prawns and egg to wok; gently stir-fry until egg sets. Add noodles, sauce mixture and remaining ingredients; stir-fry gently until hot.

SERVES 4

per serving 24g fat; 2486kJ

tip Palm sugar, also sold as jaggery, is a product of the coconut palm. It is available from Asian grocery stores, but you can substitute black or brown sugar if unavailable.

serving suggestion Sprinkle pad thai with extra chopped peanuts to serve. Traditionally, this dish is accompanied with a soup such as tom yum goong, which is consumed like a beverage throughout the meal.

nasi goreng

PREPARATION TIME 10 MINUTES • COOKING TIME 10 MINUTES

Nasi goreng is the Indonesian term for fried rice – easily made using leftover white rice.
Shrimp paste, also known as trasi and blachan, is available from Asian grocery stores and selected
supermarkets. You will need to cook about 1¹/₂ cups (300g) long-grain white rice for this recipe.

1 small brown onion (100g),
   chopped coarsely
2 cloves garlic, quartered
1 teaspoon shrimp paste
2 tablespoons peanut oil
4 eggs
125g small shelled
   uncooked prawns
4 cups (600g) cold, cooked
   long-grain white rice
3 green onions, sliced thinly
125g Chinese barbecued pork,
   sliced thinly
2 tablespoons light soy sauce

1 Blend or process brown onion, garlic and paste until almost smooth.

2 Heat half of the oil in medium frying pan; break eggs into pan. Cook, uncovered, until egg white has set and yolk is cooked as desired.

3 Meanwhile, heat remaining oil in wok or large frying pan; stir-fry onion mixture until fragrant. Add prawns; stir-fry until prawns just change colour.

4 Add rice, green onion, pork and sauce; stir-fry until hot. Serve nasi goreng with eggs.

SERVES 4

per serving 19.9g fat; 1927kJ

tip To save time, freeze single-cup portions of cooked rice and defrost only what you need for each meal.

serving suggestion Serve with a salad such as gado gado (page 38), or with prawn crackers and stir-fried Asian greens.

hokkien noodle stir-fry

PREPARATION TIME 15 MINUTES • COOKING TIME 15 MINUTES

Hokkien (or stir-fry) noodles are sold in cryovac packages in the refrigerated section of your supermarket. They should be rinsed under hot water to remove starch and excess oil before use.

500g hokkien noodles
1 tablespoon peanut oil
1 teaspoon sesame oil
500g beef fillet, sliced thinly
1 medium brown onion (150g), sliced thickly
1 clove garlic, crushed
2 teaspoons grated fresh ginger
1 medium red capsicum (200g), sliced thinly
1 medium green capsicum (200g), sliced thinly
2 tablespoons lemon juice
2 tablespoons sweet chilli sauce
1 tablespoon sesame seeds, toasted
1 tablespoon finely chopped fresh coriander
1 tablespoon finely chopped fresh mint

1 Rinse noodles under hot water; drain. Transfer to large bowl; separate noodles with fork.

2 Meanwhile, heat both oils in wok or large frying pan; stir-fry beef, in batches, until browned all over.

3 Add onion, garlic and ginger to wok; stir-fry until onion softens. Add capsicums; stir-fry until just tender.

4 Return beef to wok with noodles, juice and sauce; stir-fry until hot. Stir in seeds and herbs.

SERVES 4

per serving 16.9g fat; 2154kJ

tips Place beef in the freezer about 1 hour before using to make it easier to slice.
Chicken or lamb can substituted for the beef, if you prefer.

serving suggestion Accompany stir-fry with a potent homemade sambal of finely chopped chillies in vinegar, if you like extra heat.

combination chow mein

PREPARATION TIME 20 MINUTES • COOKING TIME 10 MINUTES

Although chow mein is traditionally made with egg noodles, you can use any noodles you like. We used packaged crunchy fried noodles – crispy egg noodles that have been deep-fried in the manufacturing process. Chinese barbecued pork is available from Asian barbecue shops. You will also need about half a small chinese cabbage for this recipe.

8 medium uncooked prawns (200g)
2 tablespoons peanut oil
250g chicken mince
100g Chinese barbecued pork, sliced thinly
1 medium carrot (120g), sliced thinly
1 medium brown onion (150g), sliced thinly
2 trimmed sticks celery (150g), sliced thinly
1 medium green capsicum (200g), sliced thinly
100g button mushrooms, sliced thinly
2 cups (140g) coarsely shredded chinese cabbage
1 cup (80g) bean sprouts
3 green onions, sliced thinly
2 teaspoons cornflour
2 tablespoons light soy sauce
2 tablespoons oyster sauce
1/2 cup (125ml) chicken stock
2 x 100g packets fried noodles

1 Shell and devein prawns, leaving tails intact.

2 Heat half of the oil in wok or large frying pan; stir-fry prawns until just changed in colour. Remove prawns from wok; cover to keep warm.

3 Add chicken to wok; stir-fry until cooked through. Add pork; stir-fry until heated through. Remove from wok; cover to keep warm.

4 Heat remaining oil in wok; stir-fry carrot and brown onion until onion softens. Add celery, capsicum and mushrooms; stir-fry until vegetables are just tender.

5 Return prawns and chicken mixture to wok with cabbage, sprouts, green onion and blended cornflour, sauces and stock; stir-fry until cabbage just wilts and sauce boils and thickens. Serve on noodles.

SERVES 4

per serving 25.1g fat; 1829kJ

tips Chinese barbecued pork has a sweet-sticky coating made from soy sauce, sherry, five-spice and hoisin sauce, and is traditionally cooked in special ovens.

You can substitute soft egg noodles for the crunchy noodles, if you prefer, but check the manufacturer's instructions regarding their preparation.

serving suggestion Accompany chow mein with a bowl of soy sauce and finely chopped fresh red chilli.

vegetarian

gado gado

PREPARATION TIME 20 MINUTES • COOKING TIME 15 MINUTES

Gado gado translates roughly as "mixed mixed", which explains the casual way that Indonesians eat this salad. Drizzle vegetables with the sauce and let everyone help themselves. Gado gado can either be served at room temperature or cold.

4 cups (320g) finely shredded
   chinese cabbage
8 baby new potatoes (320g)
2 trimmed corn cobs (500g),
   sliced thickly
200g green beans, halved
1 large carrot (180g),
   sliced thinly
2 lebanese cucumbers (260g),
   sliced diagonally
1 small pineapple (800g),
   chopped coarsely
2 cups (160g) bean sprouts
150g fried tofu, chopped coarsely
4 hard-boiled eggs, halved

PEANUT SAUCE
1$^{1}/_{3}$ cups (375g) crunchy
   peanut butter
1 cup (250ml) chicken stock
2 tablespoons light soy sauce
1 tablespoon lemon juice
1 teaspoon sambal oelek
1 clove garlic, crushed
2 teaspoons sugar
$^{1}/_{2}$ cup (125ml) coconut milk

1 Boil, steam or microwave cabbage, potatoes, corn, beans and carrot, separately, until vegetables are just tender. Chop potatoes coarsely.

2 Arrange cooked vegetables, cucumber, pineapple, sprouts, tofu and egg on serving platter. Serve gado gado with peanut sauce.

peanut sauce Combine peanut butter, stock, sauce, juice, sambal, garlic and sugar in medium saucepan; bring to a boil. Reduce heat; simmer, stirring, about 1 minute or until sauce thickens slightly. Add coconut milk; stir until hot. Pour sauce into serving bowl.

SERVES 4

per serving 63.4g fat; 4065kJ

tip We used packaged fried tofu, available from supermarkets; however, you can shallow-fry cubes of firm tofu in vegetable oil until browned lightly, then drain on absorbent paper, if preferred.

serving suggestion Serve as a light lunch with freshly puffed prawn crackers, or as a more substantial meal with boiled rice and a meat dish.

eggplant egg foo yung

PREPARATION TIME 15 MINUTES • COOKING TIME 10 MINUTES

Chinese omelettes are simple to prepare and make a delicious breakfast or light lunch.
In this vegetarian version, we've used bean sprouts, green onion and baby eggplant,
but you can substitute any combination of vegetables you like.

1 cup (250ml) chicken stock
1 tablespoon oyster sauce
1 tablespoon dry sherry
1 tablespoon cornflour
1/4 cup (60ml) water
10 eggs, beaten lightly
4 cups (320g) bean sprouts,
    chopped coarsely
4 green onions, sliced thinly
1 red thai chilli, chopped finely
2 baby eggplants (120g),
    chopped finely
1 tablespoon peanut oil

1 Combine stock, sauce and sherry in small saucepan; bring to a boil. Stir in blended cornflour and water; bring to a boil, stirring, until sauce boils and thickens.

2 Combine egg, sprouts, onion, chilli and eggplant in large bowl.

3 Heat oil in large frying pan; add 1/2 cup of the egg mixture. Flatten egg mixture using a spatula; cook, uncovered, until browned and set underneath. Turn; cook other side. Repeat with remaining egg mixture; you will get eight omelettes. Divide omelettes among serving dishes; drizzle with sauce before serving.

SERVES 4

per serving 18.2g fat; 1157kJ

tip If you find it difficult to flip omelettes, you can place the frying pan under a heated grill until the mixture is set and browned on top.

serving suggestion Serve alone as a light lunch or as a starter before a seafood main, such as stir-fried seafood with Asian greens (page 62).

masoor dhal with vegetables

PREPARATION TIME 15 MINUTES • COOKING TIME 20 MINUTES

Masoor dhal is the Indian name of the common red lentil found in your local supermarket. Feel free to
substitute any of your favourite vegetables if you prefer them to the ones suggested in this recipe.

1 tablespoon peanut oil
2 medium brown onions (300g),
    sliced thinly
2 medium carrots (240g),
    chopped coarsely
2 tablespoons hot curry paste
3 cups (750ml) water
2 cups (200g) cauliflower florets
3 baby eggplants (180g),
    chopped coarsely
2 medium zucchini (240g),
    chopped coarsely
3/4 cup (150g) red lentils
100g green beans, halved
2 tablespoons coarsely chopped
    fresh coriander

1 Heat oil in large saucepan; cook onion and carrot, stirring, until onion softens. Add curry paste; cook, stirring, until fragrant.

2 Add the water and cauliflower; bring to a boil. Add eggplant, zucchini and lentils; return to a boil. Reduce heat; simmer, uncovered, about 15 minutes or until lentils are tender.

3 Add beans; cook, stirring, until beans are tender. Stir in coriander.

SERVES 4

per serving 9.5g fat; 1017kJ

tip This recipe can actually be made as a lentil vegetable soup with the addition of more water or, even better, vegetable stock.

serving suggestion Serve with pappadums, puffed in a microwave oven, and steamed white rice.

green curry vegetables

PREPARATION TIME 20 MINUTES • COOKING TIME 20 MINUTES

Broccolini is milder and sweeter than traditional broccoli, is completely edible from flower to stem, and has a delicate flavour with a subtle, peppery edge. It is a cross between broccoli and chinese kale (also known as chinese broccoli or gai larn). You'll need 1 bunch of broccolini for this recipe.

100g snake beans
1 tablespoon peanut oil
1 medium brown onion (150g),
    sliced thinly
3 kaffir lime leaves,
    shredded finely
2 tablespoons green curry paste
1 medium carrot (120g),
    sliced thinly
2 baby eggplants (120g),
    sliced thickly
3¼ cups (810ml) light
    coconut milk
100g button mushrooms,
    sliced thinly
4 medium yellow patty-pan
    squash (120g), quartered
280g broccolini, chopped coarsely
1 small red capsicum (150g),
    sliced thinly
230g can sliced bamboo
    shoots, drained
350g butternut pumpkin,
    sliced thinly

1 Cut beans into 5cm lengths.

2 Heat oil in large saucepan; cook onion and lime leaves, stirring, until onion softens. Stir in paste; cook, stirring, until fragrant. Add carrot and eggplant; cook, uncovered, until eggplant is just tender.

3 Add coconut milk; bring to a boil. Reduce heat; add mushrooms and squash. Simmer, uncovered, until squash is just tender. Add remaining ingredients; return to a boil. Reduce heat; simmer, stirring, about 5 minutes or until vegetables are tender.

SERVES 4

per serving 21.3g fat; 1293kJ

tips Commercially prepared green curry pastes can vary in strength from mild to mouth-searing, so you may need to adjust the amount used.

We used light coconut milk to reduce the fat count in this recipe; you can use regular coconut milk if you prefer.

serving suggestion Serve this curry with steamed jasmine rice.

vegetable and lentil sambar

PREPARATION TIME 15 MINUTES • COOKING TIME 30 MINUTES

A sambar is a South-Indian dish made of a combination of dhal and vegetables. Dhal is the Indian term for pulses – lentils, dried peas and beans – as well as the spicy stew-like dishes that contain them. In this recipe, we've used yellow split peas (toor dhal), but you can use split red lentils or chickpeas, if you prefer.

1/2 cup (100g) yellow split peas
21/2 cups (625ml) water
1 tablespoon ghee
1 teaspoon yellow mustard seeds
1/2 teaspoon ground turmeric
1/4 teaspoon chilli flakes
11/2 teaspoons ground cumin
16 dried curry leaves
700g butternut pumpkin,
    chopped coarsely
2 medium carrots (240g),
    quartered lengthways,
    sliced thickly
2 cups (200g) cauliflower florets
1 tablespoon cornflour
1 tablespoon water, extra
12/3 cups (410ml) coconut milk
1 cup (125g) frozen peas, thawed

1 Combine split peas and 11/2 cups (375ml) of the water in medium saucepan. Bring to a boil; reduce heat. Simmer, uncovered, about 10 minutes or until split peas are tender; drain.

2 Meanwhile, melt ghee in large saucepan; cook seeds, spices and curry leaves, stirring, until fragrant. Add the remaining water; bring to a boil. Reduce heat; add pumpkin, carrot and cauliflower. Simmer, covered, about 10 minutes or until vegetables are just tender.

3 Stir in blended cornflour, extra water and coconut milk; bring to a boil, stirring, until sauce boils and thickens.

4 Just before serving, add split peas and peas; cook, stirring, until hot.

SERVES 4

per serving 27g fat; 1579kJ

tips Ghee, or clarified butter, has the milk solids removed and can be heated to much higher temperatures than butter without burning. It's available at many supermarkets but, if you can't buy it, you can make your own by melting butter gently and using only the oil that comes to the top.

This recipe can be made a day ahead and refrigerated, covered.

serving suggestion Steamed basmati rice and warm naan turn this dish into a meal.

spiced rice and lentils with caramelised onions

PREPARATION TIME 10 MINUTES • COOKING TIME 25 MINUTES

This recipe is an adaptation of a popular Indian rice and lentil dish called kitcheree (later anglicised into the smoked-fish-and-rice dish we know as kedgeree). Red lentils don't need overnight soaking so they're quick and easy to cook.

1.25 litres (5 cups) water
1 teaspoon salt
1¹/₂ cups (300g) red lentils
1 cup (200g) basmati rice
80g butter
1 large brown onion (200g),
   sliced thinly
2 tablespoons brown sugar
¹/₄ teaspoon ground coriander
¹/₄ teaspoon ground turmeric
¹/₄ teaspoon ground cardamom
¹/₂ teaspoon ground cumin
¹/₄ teaspoon ground black pepper
2 tablespoons finely chopped
   fresh flat-leaf parsley

1 Combine the water and salt in large saucepan; bring to a boil. Add lentils and rice; cook, uncovered, about 15 minutes or until liquid is absorbed. Remove from heat; stand, covered, 5 minutes.

2 Meanwhile, melt half of the butter in medium frying pan; cook onion and sugar, stirring, about 10 minutes or until onion caramelises.

3 Melt remaining butter; combine with spices in small bowl. Stir into rice mixture with parsley.

4 Serve lentil mixture topped with onion mixture.

SERVES 4

per serving 18.3g fat; 2331kJ

tips For a more substantial dish, add vegetables such as potatoes, cauliflower or carrots.

This recipe can be prepared a day ahead and refrigerated, covered.

serving suggestion Serve this dish with balti fish curry (page 54) or pork vindaloo (page 94), and accompany with bowls of yogurt or fruit chutney.

hoisin vegetable stir-fry

PREPARATION TIME 15 MINUTES • COOKING TIME 10 MINUTES

When you're short on time, an easy vegetable stir-fry is the ideal meal.
You will need half a small chinese cabbage for this recipe.

500g fresh rice noodles
1½ tablespoons peanut oil
2 eggs, beaten lightly
2 teaspoons sesame oil
1 medium carrot (120g),
  sliced thinly
1 small red capsicum (150g),
  sliced thinly
1 cup (80g) bean sprouts
3 cups (210g) shredded
  chinese cabbage
4 green onions, sliced thinly
¼ cup (60ml) hoisin sauce
1 tablespoon light soy sauce
2 teaspoons sambal oelek

1 Rinse noodles under hot water; drain. Transfer to large bowl; separate noodles with fork.

2 Brush heated wok or large frying pan with a little of the peanut oil. Add egg; swirl to cover base of wok. Cook, covered, about 3 minutes or until cooked through. Roll omelette tightly; slice thinly.

3 Heat sesame oil in same wok; stir-fry carrot until just tender. Add capsicum, sprouts, cabbage and onion; stir-fry until just tender. Remove vegetables; keep warm.

4 Heat remaining peanut oil in same wok; stir-fry noodles, sauces and sambal until sauce thickens and noodles are heated through. Return vegetables to wok; stir-fry until hot.

5 Serve stir-fry topped with omelette.

SERVES 4

per serving 13.9g fat; 1746kJ

tip You could substitute dried noodles for fresh noodles, if you prefer. Dried noodles should be soaked in boiling water to soften them before use.

serving suggestion This stir-fry would be great served with grilled or barbecued chicken or seafood.

fried tofu and green vegetables

PREPARATION TIME 15 MINUTES • COOKING TIME 15 MINUTES

*We used packaged fried tofu which you can buy from many supermarkets. However,
if you prefer to do it yourself, you can shallow-fry cubes of firm tofu in vegetable oil
until browned lightly, then drain on absorbent paper.*

1 tablespoon peanut oil

**1 large brown onion (200g),
sliced thickly**

2 cloves garlic, crushed

1 tablespoon grated fresh ginger

2 red thai chillies, chopped finely

200g green beans

250g asparagus

500g baby bok choy, quartered

500g choy sum, chopped coarsely

1 tablespoon fish sauce

2 tablespoons sweet chilli sauce

2 tablespoons brown sugar

1/4 cup (60ml) lime juice

300g fried tofu

**1/4 cup loosely packed, coarsely
chopped fresh coriander**

**1/4 cup loosely packed, coarsely
chopped fresh mint**

1 Heat oil in wok or large frying pan; stir-fry onion, garlic, ginger and chilli until onion just softens.

2 Add beans and asparagus; stir-fry until tender. Add bok choy, choy sum, sauces, sugar and juice; stir-fry until bok choy just wilts. Add tofu and herbs; stir-fry until hot.

SERVES 4

per serving 9.9g fat; 850kJ

tip Most vegetables can be stir-fried successfully, but ensure they are as dry as possible before cooking to prevent them becoming soggy.

serving suggestion Serve this dish as a main meal, after a starter of vegetarian spring rolls.

vietnamese omelette

PREPARATION TIME 10 MINUTES (plus standing time) • COOKING TIME 15 MINUTES

We used vietnamese mint in this recipe, a narrow-leafed pungent herb used in South-East Asia to flavour everything from spring rolls and soups to salads and Singaporean laksa, but you can use whatever kind of mint is available.

5 dried shiitake mushrooms
8 eggs
1/2 cup (125ml) milk
1 tablespoon finely chopped fresh vietnamese mint
1 tablespoon peanut oil
5 green onions, sliced thinly
2 cloves garlic, crushed
230g can sliced bamboo shoots, drained
1 medium carrot (120g), sliced thinly
1 large red capsicum (350g), sliced thinly
1 cup (80g) bean sprouts
1 tablespoon mild chilli sauce
2 tablespoons light soy sauce
1 tablespoon finely chopped fresh coriander

1 Place mushrooms in small heatproof bowl; cover with boiling water. Stand 20 minutes; drain. Discard stems; slice caps thinly.

2 Meanwhile, whisk eggs, milk and mint in medium bowl until combined.

3 Heat half of the oil in medium frying pan; cook onion, garlic and bamboo shoots, stirring, until onion softens. Add carrot and capsicum; cook, stirring, until carrot is just tender. Add mushrooms, sprouts, sauces and coriander; cook, stirring, until heated through. Remove from pan; keep warm.

4 Heat remaining oil in pan. Add a quarter of the egg mixture; cook over medium heat, tilting pan, until egg mixture is almost set. Place a quarter of the vegetable mixture evenly over half of the omelette. Fold omelette over to enclose filling; slide onto serving plate. Repeat with remaining egg and vegetable mixtures.

SERVES 4

per serving 16.7g fat; 1077kJ

tip You can add water chestnuts to this omelette for extra crunch or fresh chilli for a hotter flavour.

serving suggestion These omelettes are delicious served with steamed bok choy.

vegetable and tofu stir-fry

PREPARATION TIME 15 MINUTES • COOKING TIME 25 MINUTES

This simple Asian dish is a great option for vegetarians as it includes tofu instead of meat.
We used vermicelli-style rice noodles in this recipe.

250g thin dried rice noodles
2 tablespoons peanut oil
2 cloves garlic, crushed
1 tablespoon grated fresh ginger
150g fried tofu
2 medium carrots (240g),
  sliced thinly
1 medium red capsicum (200g),
  sliced thinly
250g chinese broccoli,
  chopped coarsely
1 tablespoon cornflour
1 tablespoon brown sugar
1/3 cup (80ml) oyster sauce
1/3 cup (80ml) light soy sauce
2 tablespoons mirin

1 Place noodles in medium heatproof bowl; cover with boiling water. Stand until just tender; drain.

2 Heat oil in wok or large frying pan; stir-fry garlic, ginger, tofu, carrot, capsicum and broccoli until vegetables are just tender.

3 Add blended cornflour, sugar, sauces and mirin; stir-fry until mixture boils and thickens. Add noodles; stir-fry until hot.

SERVES 4

per serving 12.5g fat; 1665kJ

tip Mirin is a sweetened rice wine used in Japanese cooking. It is sometimes referred to simply as rice wine, but should not be confused with sake, the Japanese rice wine made for drinking. You can substitute sweet white wine or sherry for mirin.

serving suggestion Serve gow gees or spring rolls as a starter.

eggs in chilli sauce

PREPARATION TIME 10 MINUTES • COOKING TIME 25 MINUTES

Sambal goreng telur, as this dish is known throughout Indonesia, is a popular recipe featuring
hard-boiled eggs in a rich sauce. The authentic recipe is extremely hot, but you can vary the
flavour to suit your tastebuds – use less chilli and more coconut milk for a milder version.

2 teaspoons chilli flakes
1 tablespoon coarsely
  chopped macadamias
2 medium brown onions (300g),
  chopped coarsely
4 cloves garlic, quartered
2 tablespoons coarsely chopped
  lemon grass
1 tablespoon peanut oil
2 cups (500ml) coconut milk
2/3 cup (160ml) vegetable stock
1 teaspoon grated fresh galangal
4 kaffir lime leaves
8 hard-boiled eggs, halved

1 Blend or process chilli, nuts, onion, garlic, lemon grass and oil until almost smooth.

2 Stir-fry chilli mixture in heated wok or large frying pan until fragrant. Add coconut milk, stock, galangal and lime leaves; bring to a boil. Reduce heat; simmer, stirring, about 5 minutes or until sauce thickens.

3 Add eggs to sauce and cook, uncovered, until hot.

SERVES 4

per serving 44.5g fat; 2157kJ

tips We used chilli flakes in this recipe but you can use sambal oelek, if you prefer. Sambal oelek is a salty paste made from ground chillies and vinegar; in Indonesia it is used as a hot relish or added to recipes as a flavouring.

Eggs can be boiled a day ahead and refrigerated, covered.

serving suggestion Serve sprinkled with coarsely chopped coriander and steamed jasmine rice.

seafood

mustard-seed chilli prawns

PREPARATION TIME 20 MINUTES • COOKING TIME 7 MINUTES

Mustard seeds are available in black, brown or yellow varieties; here, we used black, as they are more spicy and piquant than the other varieties. You can purchase mustard seeds from major supermarkets or health food shops.

20 large uncooked prawns (1kg)
1/4 teaspoon ground turmeric
2 red thai chillies, seeded,
**   chopped finely**
2 tablespoons vegetable oil
2 teaspoons black mustard seeds
2 cloves garlic, crushed
2 tablespoons finely chopped
**   fresh coriander**

1 Shell and devein prawns, leaving tails intact. Cut along back of prawn, taking care not to cut all the way through; flatten prawn slightly.

2 Rub turmeric and chilli into prawns in medium bowl.

3 Heat oil in large frying pan; cook mustard seeds and garlic, stirring, until seeds start to pop. Add prawn mixture; cook, stirring, until prawns just change colour. Mix in coriander.

SERVES 4

per serving 10.1g fat; 823kJ

tip If you like hot dishes, don't seed the chillies before chopping, as removing the seeds and membranes lessens the heat level.

serving suggestion Serve mustard-seed chilli prawns with saffron rice. Garnish with spring onion curls.

balti fish curry

PREPARATION TIME 15 MINUTES • COOKING TIME 25 MINUTES

There is some controversy over the origin of balti cooking, but regardless of whether it was Indian, Pakistani or Bangladeshi, the method is the same. Traditionally, a cast-iron wok-like pan, called a karahi, is used to quickly stir-fry ingredients. A wok or large frying pan is a perfect substitute.

800g white fish fillets
1 tablespoon vegetable oil
3 medium white onions (450g),
  sliced thinly
2 cloves garlic, crushed
1 tablespoon grated fresh ginger
1 red thai chilli, chopped finely
2 teaspoons ground turmeric
1 teaspoon sweet paprika
1 teaspoon ground cumin
2 x 400g cans whole
  peeled tomatoes
1/4 cup (60ml) coconut cream
1/4 cup loosely packed, finely
  chopped fresh coriander
1 tablespoon finely chopped
  fresh mint

1 Cut fish into 2cm pieces.

2 Heat oil in wok or large frying pan; cook onion, garlic, ginger, chilli and spices until onion softens.

3 Add undrained crushed tomatoes to onion mixture; bring to a boil. Reduce heat; simmer, uncovered, about 10 minutes or until sauce thickens slightly.

4 Add fish and coconut cream; bring to a boil. Reduce heat; simmer, uncovered, about 10 minutes or until fish is cooked through. Just before serving, stir coriander and mint into curry.

SERVES 4

per serving 12.9g fat; 1491kJ

tip If you don't like hot flavours, seed the chilli; if you like your food spicy, then pop in an extra chilli.

serving suggestion Serve with warm naan and steamed basmati rice (or a pilaf) garnished with mint.

spicy fish kebabs

PREPARATION TIME 15 MINUTES • COOKING TIME 15 MINUTES

We've used lemon grass stems as skewers in this recipe because they impart a fresh tangy
flavour to the fish, but you can use bamboo skewers if you prefer.

1kg firm white fish fillets
1 tablespoon coarsely chopped
  fresh mint
1 tablespoon coarsely chopped
  fresh coriander
1 tablespoon coarsely chopped
  fresh flat-leaf parsley
2 red thai chillies, chopped finely
2 tablespoons lemon juice
1 tablespoon peanut oil
4 x 30cm-long lemon grass stems

1 Cut fish into 2cm pieces.

2 Combine fish with herbs, chilli, juice and oil in medium bowl.

3 Cut lemon grass stems in half crossways; thread fish onto lemon grass skewers.

4 Cook fish on heated oiled grill plate (or grill or barbecue) until browned all over and cooked through.

SERVES 4

per serving 10.1g fat; 1251kJ

tip If using bamboo skewers, soak skewers in water for at least 1 hour before using to prevent them scorching and splintering during cooking.

serving suggestion Serve this dish on a bed of crispy potato slices. Accompany with lemon wedges.

steamed coconut fish

PREPARATION TIME 10 MINUTES • COOKING TIME 25 MINUTES

We used snapper in this recipe, but you can use any whole white-fleshed fish, such as bream or flathead. You will need a piece of ginger about 3cm long for this recipe.

2 cups coarsely chopped fresh coriander
2 red thai chillies, coarsely chopped
2 cloves garlic, quartered
20g fresh ginger, peeled, chopped coarsely
1 tablespoon cumin seeds
2/3 cup (50g) shredded coconut
1 tablespoon peanut oil
4 medium whole snapper (1.8kg)

1 Blend or process coriander, chilli, garlic, ginger and seeds until chopped finely.

2 Combine coriander mixture with coconut and oil in small bowl; mix well.

3 Score each fish three times on both sides; place fish on a large sheet of foil. Press coconut mixture onto fish; fold foil over to enclose fish.

4 Place fish in large bamboo steamer; steam fish, covered, over wok or large saucepan of simmering water about 25 minutes or until cooked through.

SERVES 4

per serving 15.8g fat; 1237kJ

tips Prick the foil with a skewer to allow the steam to escape.

Don't know how to score fish? It simply means making shallow cuts in the fish, often in a criss-cross pattern, to allow the herbs and spices to penetrate the flesh and enhance the flavour.

serving suggestion Serve with steamed long-grain white rice and stir-fried bok choy with ginger and garlic.

chilli scallops

PREPARATION TIME 15 MINUTES • COOKING TIME 15 MINUTES

We used scallops with roe in this recipe; but the roe can be left out if you prefer.
You will need a piece of ginger about 5cm long for this recipe.

1 tablespoon peanut oil
32 small scallops
4 cloves garlic, sliced thinly
50g fresh ginger, peeled,
   sliced thinly
2 red thai chillies, seeded,
   chopped finely
3 green onions, sliced thinly
1/3 cup (80ml) sweet chilli sauce
1 teaspoon fish sauce
2 teaspoons brown sugar
1/2 cup (125ml) chicken stock
1/4 cup loosely packed, coarsely
   chopped fresh coriander

1 Heat half of the oil in wok or large frying pan; stir-fry scallops, in batches, until just changed in colour.

2 Heat remaining oil in wok; stir-fry garlic, ginger, chilli and onion until onion is soft.

3 Stir in combined sauces, sugar and stock; bring to a boil. Return scallops to wok; stir until heated through. Serve scallops sprinkled with coriander.

SERVES 4

per serving 6.1g fat; 585kJ

tip If you buy scallops in their shell, don't discard the shell, they are great (washed and dried) to use as serving "dishes" for the chilli scallops.

serving suggestion Serve with steamed jasmine rice and a bowl of finely chopped chilli for extra bite.

salt and pepper squid

PREPARATION 15 MINUTES • COOKING TIME 5 MINUTES

*In China, this dish is usually enjoyed as a starter, but when you add boiled rice
and wilted Asian greens it makes a substantial main meal.*

500g squid hoods
3/4 cup (110g) plain flour
2 tablespoons salt
2 tablespoons ground
 black pepper
vegetable oil, for deep-frying
150g mesclun

CHILLI DRESSING

1/2 cup (125ml) sweet chilli sauce
1 teaspoon fish sauce
1/4 cup (60ml) lime juice
1 clove garlic, crushed

1 Cut squid in half lengthways; score inside surface of each piece.
 Cut into 2cm-wide strips.

2 Combine flour, salt and pepper in large bowl; add squid. Coat in flour
 mixture; shake off excess.

3 Heat oil in wok or large saucepan; deep-fry squid, in batches, until
 tender and browned all over. Drain on absorbent paper.

4 Serve squid on mesclun with chilli dressing.

chilli dressing Combine sauces, juice and garlic in screw-topped jar;
shake well.

SERVES 4

per serving 12.2g fat; 1375kJ

tip Place flour, salt and pepper in a strong plastic bag with squid; grip the
bag tightly closed, then gently shake to coat the squid in flour mixture.
Remove squid from bag, shaking off any excess flour.

serving suggestion Serve with wedges of lime or lemon for added piquancy.

lemon grass and lime fish parcels

PREPARATION TIME 10 MINUTES • COOKING TIME 20 MINUTES

*The lemon grass in this dish is not eaten, but it produces an amazing aroma
and flavour simply by being close to the fish during cooking.*

2 lemon grass stems
1/2 cup loosely packed, coarsely
    chopped fresh coriander
1 teaspoon grated fresh ginger
3 cloves garlic, crushed
4 spring onions (100g),
    sliced thinly
2 red thai chillies, seeded,
    chopped finely
4 firm white fish fillets (1kg)
1 lime, sliced thinly
1 tablespoon vegetable oil

1 Trim lemon grass into 10cm pieces; cut each piece in half lengthways.

2 Combine, coriander, ginger, garlic, onion and chilli in small bowl.

3 Divide lemon grass among four pieces of foil; top with fish. Top fish
  with coriander mixture and lime; drizzle with oil.

4 Fold foil around fish to enclose completely.

5 Cook parcels on heated grill plate (or in moderate oven) about
  15 minutes or until fish is cooked through.

6 To serve, remove fish from foil and discard lemon grass.

SERVES 4

per serving 10.3g fat; 1290kJ

tip The fish can also be wrapped in blanched banana leaves.
serving suggestion Serve with steamed coconut rice and slices of lemon.

prawn sambal

PREPARATION TIME 20 MINUTES • COOKING TIME 10 MINUTES

*Despite its name, this is a main dish, not a relish. In South-East Asia, the word sambal
describes relishes, sauces and other accompaniments that are based on chilli. In Indonesia,
however, a sambal can also be a main dish, as is the case here.*

40 medium uncooked prawns (1kg)
1 tablespoon peanut oil
1 large brown onion (200g),
    chopped finely
2 cloves garlic, crushed
2 teaspoons grated fresh ginger
1 tablespoon finely chopped
    lemon grass
415g can whole peeled tomatoes
1 tablespoon sambal oelek
2 teaspoons lemon juice
1 teaspoon sugar
1 medium red capsicum (200g),
    chopped finely

1 Shell and devein prawns, leaving tails intact.

2 Heat oil in large frying pan; cook onion, garlic, ginger and lemon grass,
  stirring, until onion softens.

3 Add undrained crushed tomatoes, sambal, juice, sugar and capsicum;
  bring to a boil. Reduce heat; simmer, uncovered, until sauce thickens.

4 Add prawns; cook, stirring, until prawns just change colour.

SERVES 4

per serving 5.8g fat; 875kJ

tip Although we only used 1 tablespoon of sambal oelek – a salty paste made
from ground chillies and vinegar – you can add more for a really fiery treat!
serving suggestion Serve this sambal with lemon-scented steamed white
rice. Top with shaved lemon rind and green onion curls.

stir-fried seafood with asian greens

PREPARATION TIME 20 MINUTES • COOKING TIME 20 MINUTES

You can use flathead, snapper, ling, bream or any other firm white fish in this recipe. You will need a piece of ginger about 5cm long.

20 medium uncooked prawns (500g)
500g squid hoods
500g firm white fish fillets
1 tablespoon peanut oil
5 green onions, chopped coarsely
2 cloves garlic, sliced thinly
50g fresh ginger, peeled, sliced thinly
500g baby bok choy, trimmed, chopped coarsely
500g choy sum, trimmed, chopped coarsely
2 tablespoons light soy sauce
2 tablespoons oyster sauce
1 tablespoon mild chilli sauce

1 Shell and devein prawns, leaving tails intact. Cut squid hoods in half. Score inside surface of each piece; cut into 5cm-wide strips. Cut fish into 3cm pieces.

2 Heat half of the oil in wok or large frying pan; stir-fry seafood, in batches, until browned all over and cooked through.

3 Heat remaining oil in wok; stir-fry onion, garlic and ginger until onion softens.

4 Return seafood to wok. Add bok choy, choy sum and combined sauces; stir-fry until greens are just wilted and heated through.

SERVES 4

per serving 9.9g fat; 1531kJ

tip For an even richer seafood experience, add scallops or crab meat to this dish.

serving suggestion Fresh egg noodles make the ideal accompaniment to this recipe.

vietnamese prawn salad

PREPARATION TIME 20 MINUTES • COOKING TIME 10 MINUTES

Noodles are an integral part of the Vietnamese diet that are enjoyed, in some form, at practically every meal. This recipe combines noodles with prawns – another popular ingredient in Vietnam. Ensure the prawns are cooked just before serving.

24 large uncooked prawns (1kg)
1 teaspoon sambal oelek
1 tablespoon grated fresh ginger
2 cloves garlic, crushed
2 tablespoons coarsely chopped
** fresh coriander**
2 tablespoons coarsely chopped
** fresh mint**
1 tablespoon peanut oil
¼ cup (60ml) light soy sauce
¼ cup (60ml) oyster sauce
250g rice vermicelli

1 Shell and devein prawns, leaving tails intact. Combine prawns with sambal oelek, ginger, garlic, and half of the fresh herbs in a large bowl.

2 Heat oil in large wok or frying pan; cook prawn mixture, in batches, stirring over high heat until prawns just change colour. Add half of the combined sauces; stir-fry until hot.

3 Place noodles in medium heatproof bowl; cover with boiling water. Stand until just tender; drain.

4 Combine noodles with remaining sauce mixture, coriander and mint. Serve noodle mixture with prawns.

SERVES 4

per serving 6.3g fat; 1526kJ

tip You can substitute bean thread noodles, also known as cellophane noodles, for rice vermicelli if you wish.

serving suggestion Serve accompanied by a bowl of soy or fish sauce.

seafood combination omelette

PREPARATION TIME 10 MINUTES • COOKING TIME 15 MINUTES

The Cantonese have a particular fondness for omelettes, and they would love this one featuring crab, prawns and scallops, all regarded with relish throughout southern China.

12 eggs, beaten lightly
4 green onions, sliced thinly
1 tablespoon vegetable oil
1 clove garlic, crushed
1 red thai chilli, seeded,
  sliced thinly
26 scallops, halved
400g small shelled cooked prawns
400g cooked crab meat
2 tablespoons light soy sauce
1/3 cup firmly packed
  fresh coriander
2 tablespoons coarsely chopped
  fresh mint

1 Whisk eggs and onion together in large bowl.

2 Brush medium heated non-stick frying pan with a little of the oil. Add a quarter of the egg mixture; swirl to cover base of pan. Cook, covered, about 3 minutes or until cooked through. Remove omelette; repeat with remaining egg mixture to make three more omelettes.

3 Meanwhile, heat remaining oil in wok or large frying pan; stir-fry garlic, chilli and scallops until scallops are cooked through.

4 Add prawns, crab, sauce and herbs; stir until heated through.

5 Divide seafood mixture among omelettes; roll to enclose filling. Cut each omelette in half diagonally.

SERVES 4

per serving 22.2g fat; 1956kJ

tip We removed the roe from the scallops, but it can be left intact, if you prefer.

serving suggestion Serve this omelette with fried rice and steamed Asian greens.

poultry

chicken tikka with cucumber-mint raita

PREPARATION TIME 15 MINUTES • COOKING TIME 10 MINUTES

*The word tikka actually refers to a bite-sized piece of meat, poultry, fish or vegetable.
Our recipe, a quick version of the popular starter in many Indian restaurants,
uses ready-made tikka paste, found in jars in most supermarkets.*

1kg chicken breast fillets, trimmed
1/2 cup (150g) tikka paste

CUCUMBER-MINT RAITA
3/4 cup (200g) yogurt
1 lebanese cucumber (130g),
   peeled, seeded, chopped finely
2 tablespoons finely chopped
   fresh mint
1 teaspoon ground cumin

1 Combine chicken with paste in large bowl.

2 Cook chicken, in batches, on heated oiled grill plate (or grill or barbecue)
  until browned all over and cooked through.

3 Serve chicken with cucumber-mint raita.

cucumber-mint raita Combine ingredients in small bowl.

SERVES 4

per serving 31.6g fat; 2148kJ

tip You can also serve this recipe in the traditional manner, by threading the
chopped or sliced chicken breast fillets onto bamboo skewers before grilling or
barbecuing. Just make certain to first soak the skewers in water for at least
1 hour to avoid them scorching and splintering during cooking.

serving suggestion Serve as a starter, on a bed of cabbage with mango chutney,
or as a main meal, with steamed basmati rice and chapatis or naan.

lemon chicken

PREPARATION TIME 15 MINUTES • COOKING TIME 15 MINUTES

This southern Chinese speciality can be baked to reduce the fat content.

**4 single chicken breast
fillets (680g)**
2 egg whites, beaten lightly
¹/₂ cup (75g) plain flour
30g butter
2 tablespoons vegetable oil
1¹/₂ tablespoons cornflour
1 tablespoon brown sugar
¹/₂ cup (125ml) lemon juice
¹/₂ teaspoon grated fresh ginger
1 teaspoon light soy sauce
1 cup (250ml) chicken stock

1 Using a meat mallet, gently pound chicken between sheets of plastic wrap until 1cm thick.

2 Dip chicken in egg white. Coat in flour; shake off excess.

3 Heat butter and oil in large frying pan; cook chicken, in batches, until browned both sides and cooked through. Drain on absorbent paper.

4 Meanwhile, blend cornflour and sugar with juice in small saucepan. Add ginger, sauce and stock; bring to a boil, stirring, until sauce boils and thickens.

5 Slice chicken; serve drizzled with sauce.

SERVES 4

per serving 25.3g fat; 2011kJ

tip Make extra quantities of lemon sauce and refrigerate, as it makes a delicious stir-fry sauce and is also good served with fish.

serving suggestion Top with shredded lemon rind and serve with lemon slices and a bowl of fried or steamed white rice.

malay chicken

PREPARATION TIME 5 MINUTES • COOKING TIME 35 MINUTES

Ayam percik, as it is known in Kelantan, Malaysia, features chicken pieces marinated in a spicy coconut sauce then grilled over coals, but it also suits oven cooking. Palm sugar is a very fine textured sugar made from the sap of the coconut palm. It is also known as gula jawa, gula melaka or jaggery; you can substitute brown or black sugar for palm sugar.

1 tablespoon ground coriander
1 tablespoon ground cumin
1 tablespoon fennel seeds
1 teaspoon ground cinnamon
1/2 teaspoon ground turmeric
**2 red thai chillies, seeded,
  chopped finely**
1/2 teaspoon tamarind concentrate
2 cloves garlic, crushed
**1 tablespoon finely chopped
  lemon grass**
2 teaspoons palm sugar
1 tablespoon peanut oil
1/2 cup (125ml) coconut cream
8 chicken thigh cutlets (1.2kg)

1 Preheat oven to hot.

2 Combine spices, chilli, tamarind, garlic, lemon grass, sugar, oil and coconut cream in large bowl; stir until mixture forms a paste.

3 Add chicken to bowl; stir to coat in paste. Place chicken on wire rack in large shallow baking dish. Bake in hot oven about 15 minutes. Cover with foil; bake about 20 minutes, or until chicken is cooked through.

SERVES 4

per serving 27g fat; 1760kJ

tip To allow the flavours to develop, marinate the chicken overnight and refrigerate, covered.

serving suggestion In Malaysia, this recipe is served with nasi kerabu (rice with fresh herbs), but plain steamed white rice or a green salad will complement this dish just as well.

yakitori chicken

Yakitori is a popular Japanese snack – tiny skewers of grilled chicken pieces, served with a dipping sauce, are consumed with sake after a hard day at the office by thousands of executives! Sometimes accompanied by mushrooms, capsicum strips, onion wedges or quail eggs, the skewers can be threaded with chicken breast or thigh fillet, chicken liver or even minced chicken gizzards. Soak bamboo skewers in water for at least 1 hour before using to avoid scorching and splintering during cooking.

1kg chicken breast fillets
1/4 cup (60ml) mirin
1/2 cup (125ml) light soy sauce
2 teaspoons grated fresh ginger
2 cloves garlic, crushed
1/4 teaspoon ground black pepper
1 tablespoon sugar

1 Cut chicken into 2cm pieces.

2 Combine chicken with remaining ingredients in large bowl. Drain chicken over small bowl; reserve marinade.

3 Thread chicken onto 12 bamboo skewers. Cook skewers on heated oiled grill plate (or grill or barbecue), turning and brushing with reserved marinade occasionally. Cook until yakitori are browned all over and cooked through.

SERVES 4

per serving 13.8g fat; 1614kJ

tip Mirin is a somewhat sweet rice wine used in many Asian, especially Japanese, dishes. You can substitute sherry or sweet white wine for mirin, if you prefer.

serving suggestion This dish is usually served as a snack with drinks in Japanese bars, rather than a main meal. You can make twice the quantity of marinade and serve half as a dipping sauce, if you like.

peking duck rice-paper rolls

PREPARATION TIME 30 MINUTES

This is a modern variation of the traditional Peking duck served in Chinese restaurants worldwide.
It has all the flavour and panache of the authentic dish but we've considerably reduced the time and
effort involved! We used a 1kg Chinese barbecued duck for this recipe.

1 Chinese barbecued duck
2 lebanese cucumbers (260g),
halved lengthways, seeded
16 x 16.5cm-square rice
paper sheets
4 green onions, sliced
thinly lengthways
50g snow pea sprouts
1/4 cup (60ml) hoisin sauce
1 tablespoon plum sauce

1 Remove skin and meat from duck. Discard bones and skin; slice meat thinly. Slice cucumber into 5cm lengths.

2 Place one sheet of rice paper in medium bowl of warm water until softened slightly; lift sheet carefully from water. Place on board; pat dry with absorbent paper. Place some of the duck, cucumber, onion, sprouts and 1 teaspoon of the combined sauces in centre of sheet.

3 Fold bottom half of the rice paper up. Fold in sides; roll over to enclose filling, allowing sprouts to come slightly above top edge. Repeat with remaining rice paper sheets and remaining ingredients.

MAKES 16

per serving 3.3g fat; 387kJ

tips Rice paper rolls can be made a day ahead and refrigerated, covered. You can also make double the quantity of combined sauces and use half as a dipping sauce.

serving suggestion These rolls can be served as a starter before a main meal of Mongolian garlic lamb (page 88).

spicy duck curry

PREPARATION TIME 5 MINUTES • COOKING TIME 15 MINUTES

We used a 1kg Chinese barbecued duck for this recipe. Traditionally cooked in special ovens,
Chinese barbecued duck has a sweet-sticky coating made from soy sauce, sherry, five-spice and hoisin sauce.
It is available from Asian food stores; ask them to chop it for you to make this recipe even easier!

cooking-oil spray
1 large brown onion (200g),
sliced thinly
2 tablespoons red curry paste
3 1/4 cups (810ml) light
coconut milk
1 Chinese barbecued duck,
chopped coarsely
150g green beans,
chopped coarsely

1 Spray large saucepan with cooking-oil spray; cook onion in heated saucepan, stirring, until onion softens.

2 Add paste; cook, stirring, until fragrant. Add coconut milk; bring to a boil. Reduce heat; simmer.

3 Add duck and beans; cook, uncovered, about 5 minutes or until beans are just tender and sauce thickens slightly.

SERVES 4

per serving 40g fat; 1994kJ

tip Different brands of commercially prepared curry pastes vary in strength and flavour, so you may want to adjust the amount of paste to suit your taste.

serving suggestion Steamed jasmine rice is a perfect partner for this dish.

garlic chicken stir-fry with bok choy

PREPARATION TIME 15 MINUTES • COOKING TIME 10 MINUTES

This is a quick and easy recipe that doesn't contain any chilli, so it's suitable for the whole family.

**750g chicken breast fillets,
   sliced thinly**
1/2 cup (75g) plain flour
2 tablespoons peanut oil
6 cloves garlic, crushed
**1 medium red capsicum (200g),
   sliced thinly**
6 green onions, sliced thinly
1/2 cup (125ml) chicken stock
2 tablespoons light soy sauce
500g bok choy, chopped coarsely

1 Coat chicken in flour; shake off excess.

2 Heat oil in wok or large frying pan; stir-fry chicken, in batches, until browned all over and cooked through.

3 Add garlic, capsicum and onion to wok; stir-fry until capsicum is tender.

4 Return chicken to wok with stock and sauce; stir-fry until sauce boils and thickens slightly. Just before serving, add bok choy; stir-fry until bok choy just wilts.

SERVES 4

per serving 20.4g fat; 1838kJ

tip You can substitute any Asian green for the bok choy.

serving suggestion This dish goes nicely with crispy fried noodles or steamed white rice.

five-spice quail and cabbage

PREPARATION TIME 20 MINUTES • COOKING TIME 10 MINUTES

We used vietnamese mint in this recipe. This narrow-leafed, pungent herb, also known as cambodian mint and laksa leaf, is widely used in South-East Asian soups and salads, but you can substitute any mint that is available. You will need about half a small chinese cabbage for this recipe.

2 medium brown onions (300g), sliced thinly
1 tablespoon salt
4 quails (780g)
1/4 cup (60ml) fish sauce
1 tablespoon light soy sauce
2 tablespoons rice wine
1 clove garlic, crushed
1 teaspoon grated fresh ginger
1 teaspoon five-spice powder
1/4 teaspoon cracked black pepper
2 tablespoons sugar
1/4 cup (60ml) lime juice
1/4 cup (60ml) white vinegar
1/3 cup loosely packed, finely chopped fresh coriander
1/3 cup loosely packed, finely chopped fresh vietnamese mint
3 cups (210g) coarsely shredded chinese cabbage

1 Combine onion and salt in small bowl.

2 Using sharp knife or scissors, cut down either side of backbone of quail; discard backbones. Gently flatten quail.

3 Combine 1 tablespoon of the fish sauce with soy sauce, wine, garlic, ginger, five-spice and pepper in large bowl. Add quail; coat well.

4 Cook quail on heated oiled grill plate (or grill or barbecue) until browned all over and cooked through.

5 Meanwhile, rinse salt from onion; drain well.

6 Combine remaining fish sauce, sugar, juice, vinegar and herbs in large bowl. Add cabbage and onion to herb mixture; mix well. Divide cabbage mixture among four plates; top with quail.

SERVES 4

per serving 17.4g fat; 1504kJ

tips Quail can be marinated overnight and refrigerated, covered.
You can substitute dry sherry for the rice wine, if you prefer.
serving suggestion Accompany quail with steamed or boiled jasmine rice.

chiang mai chicken salad

PREPARATION TIME 15 MINUTES • COOKING TIME 5 MINUTES

The north-western province around Chiang Mai in Thailand is famous for its delicious
chicken salad, called larb; it can also be made with beef or pork mince.

1kg chicken mince
1 tablespoon long-grain white rice
1 teaspoon sesame oil
1/3 cup (80ml) lime juice
1 tablespoon fish sauce
1 tablespoon light soy sauce
4 green onions, sliced thinly
2 red thai chillies, seeded,
   sliced thinly
1 tablespoon finely chopped
   lemon grass
1/4 cup loosely packed, coarsely
   chopped fresh mint
1/4 cup loosely packed, coarsely
   chopped fresh coriander leaves
1 teaspoon finely chopped fresh
   coriander root
4 medium iceberg lettuce leaves

1   Cook chicken in large saucepan with 2 tablespoons water, stirring, until changed in colour; drain.

2   Heat dry wok; cook rice, stirring, until golden brown. Remove from heat; cool. Blend or process rice until rice resembles a fine powder.

3   Combine chicken and rice with oil, juice, sauces, onion, chilli, lemon grass and herbs in large bowl.

4   Divide larb among lettuce leaves.

SERVES 4

per serving   21.6g fat; 1729kJ

tip   You can substitute leftover roast or barbecued chicken for the chicken mince if you prefer, but ensure you dice the flesh very finely.

serving suggestion   Serve as a starter, with lime wedges, before a light seafood main meal, such as lemon grass and lime fish parcels (page 60).

lemon grass chicken

PREPARATION TIME 10 MINUTES • COOKING TIME 35 MINUTES

The intense aroma and flavour of lemon grass is an essential ingredient in myriad Asian dishes – from soups and salads to curries and stir-fries. Its widespread appeal means you can find it in most supermarkets but, when slicing or chopping, ensure you use only the white section of the stem. Lovely legs are trimmed, skinned chicken drumsticks.

8 chicken lovely legs (960g)
2 tablespoons finely chopped lemon grass
4 spring onions (100g), chopped finely
2 teaspoons fish sauce
1 teaspoon sambal oelek
1 teaspoon sugar
1 tablespoon peanut oil

1 Preheat oven to moderately hot.

2 Combine ingredients in baking dish.

3 Bake, uncovered, in moderately hot oven about 35 minutes or until chicken is cooked through, turning chicken once during cooking.

SERVES 4

per serving 15.1g fat; 1084kJ

tip You can use any cut of chicken you wish in this recipe.

serving suggestion Coconut rice and steamed chinese broccoli – drizzled with warmed sesame oil and oyster sauce – turn this dish into a satisfying main meal.

butter chicken

PREPARATION TIME 5 MINUTES • COOKING TIME 25 MINUTES

In India, chicken is regarded as a delicacy, and the mouth-watering flavour of butter chicken,
also known as murgh makhani, is a real treat. This famous dish, featuring chicken simmered
in a rich, creamy tomato and butter sauce, is a delicious addition to any Indian banquet.

80g butter
1 medium brown onion (150g),
  chopped finely
3 cloves garlic, crushed
3 teaspoons sweet paprika
2 teaspoons garam masala
2 teaspoons ground coriander
1/2 teaspoon chilli powder
1 cinnamon stick
2 tablespoons white vinegar
425g can tomato puree
3/4 cup (180ml) chicken stock
1 tablespoon tomato paste
750g chicken thigh
  fillets, quartered
1 cup (250ml) cream
1/2 cup (140g) yogurt

1 Melt butter in large saucepan; cook onion, garlic and spices, stirring, until onion softens.

2 Add vinegar, puree, stock and paste; bring to a boil. Reduce heat; simmer, uncovered, for 10 minutes, stirring occasionally.

3 Add chicken to pan with cream and yogurt; bring to a boil. Reduce heat; simmer, uncovered, about 10 minutes or until chicken is cooked through.

SERVES 4

per serving 59.2g fat; 3124kJ

tip In India, this dish is often made using leftover tandoori chicken pieces; it can also be made using chicken breast fillets, if you prefer.

serving suggestion Serve butter chicken with cucumber raita, boiled or steamed basmati rice and warm naan bread.

barbecued duck and noodle stir-fry

PREPARATION TIME 15 MINUTES • COOKING TIME 20 MINUTES

We used a 1kg Chinese barbecued duck for this recipe, available from Asian barbecue takeaway stores; ask them to chop the duck for you.

600g hokkien noodles
1 tablespoon peanut oil
2 cloves garlic, crushed
150g sugar snap peas
1 large red capsicum (350g), sliced thinly
1 Chinese barbecued duck, chopped coarsely
450g baby bok choy, chopped coarsely
1 tablespoon light soy sauce
1/4 cup (60ml) hoisin sauce
1/4 cup (60ml) chicken stock

1 Rinse noodles under hot water; drain. Transfer to large bowl; separate noodles with fork.

2 Meanwhile, heat oil in wok or large frying pan; stir-fry garlic, peas and capsicum until capsicum is just tender.

3 Add noodles, duck, bok choy, sauces and stock; stir-fry until duck is heated through and bok choy wilts.

SERVES 4

per serving 33.1g fat; 2902kJ

tip You can use fresh egg or fresh rice noodles in place of the hokkien noodles, if you prefer.

serving suggestion Accompany this stir-fry with a side dish of chopped fresh chilli and coriander.

indonesian chicken curry

PREPARATION TIME 15 MINUTES • COOKING TIME 15 MINUTES

This coconut chicken curry is the ideal choice for people who don't like fiery curries.

1 tablespoon peanut oil
750g chicken thigh fillets,
    chopped coarsely
1 large brown onion (200g),
    sliced thickly
1 red thai chilli, seeded,
    chopped finely
2 cloves garlic, crushed
1 tablespoon grated fresh ginger
1 tablespoon finely chopped
    macadamia nuts
1 tablespoon ground coriander
1 teaspoon ground cumin
1/2 teaspoon ground fennel
1 cinnamon stick
31/4 cups (800ml) coconut cream
1 tablespoon lemon juice

1 Heat half of the oil in large frying pan; cook chicken, in batches, until browned all over and cooked through.

2 Heat remaining oil in pan; cook onion, chilli, garlic and ginger, stirring, until onion softens. Add nuts and spices; cook, stirring, until fragrant.

3 Return chicken to pan with coconut cream and juice; bring to a boil. Reduce heat; simmer, uncovered, about 5 minutes or until sauce thickens slightly.

SERVES 4

per serving 62g fat; 3158kJ

tip Keep fresh chillies in your freezer. Not only will you have some on hand whenever you need them, but they're easier to slice and chop while frozen.

serving suggestion Accompany this curry with steamed or boiled long-grain rice and stir-fried Asian greens. Garnish curry with thinly sliced thai chilli.

steamed chicken breasts with lime

PREPARATION TIME 10 MINUTES • COOKING TIME 20 MINUTES

This is a simple Asian dish that's not only quick, it's also low in fat. Sake is dry rice wine; it can be replaced with dry sherry or white wine if unavailable.

12 kaffir lime leaves,
    shredded finely
1/3 cup (80ml) lime juice
2 teaspoons grated fresh ginger
4 single chicken breasts (680g)
400g chinese broccoli, quartered

SOY AND GARLIC DIPPING SAUCE
2 tablespoons light soy sauce
2 tablespoons sake
2 tablespoons mild chilli sauce
1 teaspoon brown sugar
1 clove garlic, crushed
1 tablespoon coarsely chopped
    fresh coriander

1 Combine lime leaves, juice and ginger in small bowl.

2 Place each chicken breast on a large sheet of foil; drizzle with lime mixture. Fold foil over loosely to enclose chicken.

3 Place chicken in large bamboo steamer; steam chicken, covered, over wok or large saucepan of simmering water about 15 minutes or until chicken is cooked through.

4 Just before serving, add broccoli to chicken in steamer; steam, covered, until broccoli just wilts. Serve chicken and broccoli with soy and garlic dipping sauce.

soy and garlic dipping sauce Combine ingredients in small bowl.

SERVES 4

per serving 9.8g fat; 1174kJ

tip You can steam the chicken in a microwave oven, without the foil, if you prefer.

serving suggestion Serve with steamed long-grain white rice.

chicken and snake beans with holy basil

PREPARATION TIME 5 MINUTES • COOKING TIME 15 MINUTES

*While basil is thought to have originated in India, it is most often used as
a culinary herb in Asia. In this dish we've used thai basil, also known as
bai kaprow or holy basil. If you can't find it, use ordinary sweet basil instead.*

700g snake beans
1 tablespoon peanut oil
880g coarsely chopped chicken thigh fillets
2 medium white onions (300g), sliced thickly
3 cloves garlic, crushed
1 teaspoon five-spice powder
1/2 cup (125ml) oyster sauce
2 tablespoons light soy sauce
1/2 cup (75g) cashew nuts, toasted
1/2 cup loosely packed holy basil leaves

1 Cut snake beans into 5cm lengths.

2 Heat half of the oil in wok or large frying pan; stir-fry chicken, in
  batches, until browned all over and cooked through.

3 Heat remaining oil in wok; stir-fry onion, garlic and five-spice until
  onion softens. Add beans; stir-fry until beans are tender. Return chicken
  to wok with sauces and nuts; stir-fry until sauce boils and thickens
  slightly. Just before serving, stir in basil.

SERVES 4

per serving 30.7g fat; 2353kJ

tip Snake beans are long, thin green beans that are Asian in origin;
if unavailable, you can use green beans.

serving suggestion This dish is excellent with either noodles or
steamed jasmine rice.

meat

teriyaki beef

PREPARATION TIME 10 MINUTES • COOKING TIME 20 MINUTES

One of the most popular Japanese grilled meat dishes, teriyaki is so easy to prepare at home. Here, we accompany it with fresh baby corn, but try it with grilled red capsicum strips or trimmed sugar snap peas, if you prefer.

1/2 cup (125ml) mirin
1/3 cup (80ml) light soy sauce
1/4 cup (50g) firmly packed
  brown sugar
1 tablespoon sake
1 tablespoon grated fresh ginger
1 clove garlic, crushed
1 teaspoon sesame oil
1 tablespoon sesame seeds
750g beef fillet, sliced thinly
300g fresh baby corn, halved
2 green onions, sliced thinly

1   Combine mirin, sauce, sugar, sake, ginger, garlic, oil and seeds in large bowl. Stir in beef and corn; stand 5 minutes.

2   Drain beef mixture over medium saucepan; reserve marinade.

3   Cook beef and corn, in batches, on heated oiled grill plate (or grill or barbecue) until browned all over and cooked as desired.

4   Meanwhile, bring marinade to a boil. Reduce heat; simmer, uncovered, 5 minutes.

5   Serve beef and corn drizzled with hot marinade; sprinkle with onion.

SERVES 4

per serving 12.7g fat; 1819kJ

tip You can substitute pork, fish or chicken for the beef, if you prefer.
serving suggestion Serve with boiled or stir-fried noodles.

mongolian garlic lamb

PREPARATION TIME 10 MINUTES • COOKING TIME 10 MINUTES

*This popular Chinese restaurant dish has its origins in the campfire-braised meats, strewn with
masses of garlic, eaten by Mongol herders in the vast expanses of the Euro-Asian steppes.*

750g lamb fillets, sliced thinly
3 cloves garlic, crushed
1/4 cup (60ml) light soy sauce
1/3 cup (80ml) sweet sherry
1 tablespoon cornflour
2 tablespoons vegetable oil
1 tablespoon brown sugar
1 teaspoon sesame oil
8 green onions, sliced thinly

1 Combine lamb, garlic, half of the sauce, half of the sherry and cornflour in large bowl; mix well.

2 Heat vegetable oil in wok or large frying pan; stir-fry lamb mixture, in batches, until browned all over.

3 Return lamb mixture to wok. Add remaining sauce, remaining sherry, sugar and sesame oil; stir-fry until sauce boils and thickens slightly. Remove from heat; stir in onion.

SERVES 4

per serving 17.2g fat; 1546kJ

tip For a livelier version, add a finely chopped red thai chilli or two to the lamb before marinating it. Lamb can be marinated a day ahead and refrigerated, covered.

serving suggestion Serve with steamed long-grain rice and stir-fried baby bok choy in ginger.

pork tonkatsu

PREPARATION TIME 15 MINUTES • COOKING TIME 10 MINUTES

Tonkatsu is a popular Japanese dish, consisting of crumbed, fried pork slices served with a thick sauce. To make your tonkatsu as authentic as possible, buy japanese breadcrumbs (panko) and japanese mustard (karashi). Both are available from Asian food stores.

4 pork butterfly steaks (800g)
2 tablespoons light soy sauce
2 tablespoons mirin
1 clove garlic, crushed
1 egg, beaten lightly
2 cups (200g) packaged
**   japanese breadcrumbs**
vegetable oil, for shallow-frying
2 tablespoons pink pickled ginger

TONKATSU SAUCE
1 tablespoon worcestershire sauce
1/3 cup (80ml) tomato sauce
1 teaspoon light soy sauce
2 tablespoons sake
1 teaspoon japanese mustard

1 Using a meat mallet, gently pound pork between sheets of plastic wrap until about 1cm thick.

2 Combine sauce, mirin and garlic in large bowl. Add pork; mix well. Dip pork in egg; coat with breadcrumbs.

3 Heat oil in large frying pan; shallow-fry pork, in batches, until browned both sides and cooked through. Drain on absorbent paper.

4 Slice pork and serve topped with ginger; serve tonkatsu sauce separately.

tonkatsu sauce Combine ingredients in small bowl; mix well.

SERVES 4

per serving 33.7g fat; 2953kJ

tip Use pork fillets in this recipe if you prefer; stale breadcrumbs and english mustard can be used if you are unable to find the Japanese versions.
serving suggestion Serve with finely shredded cabbage and steamed rice.

spicy pork ribs

PREPARATION TIME 10 MINUTES • COOKING TIME 20 MINUTES

Ask your butcher to cut the pork ribs "American-style" so that as much fat as possible has been removed, leaving only tender, flavoursome meat.

1.5kg trimmed pork spare rib slabs
3/4 cup (180ml) light soy sauce
1 egg, beaten lightly
1/4 cup (35g) plain flour
2 tablespoons vegetable oil
1/2 cup (125ml) rice wine
1/2 cup (100g) firmly packed brown sugar
1/4 cup yellow mustard seeds
1/3 cup loosely packed, coarsely chopped fresh coriander
3 cloves garlic, crushed
1 tablespoon grated fresh ginger
3 teaspoons dried chilli flakes
1 teaspoon five-spice powder
1/2 teaspoon cayenne pepper

1 Cut slabs into individual-rib pieces.

2 Place ribs in large saucepan. Cover with water; bring to a boil. Reduce heat; simmer, uncovered, about 10 minutes or until ribs are almost cooked through. Drain; pat dry with absorbent paper.

3 Blend 1/4 cup (60ml) of the sauce, egg and flour in large bowl. Add ribs; stir to coat in soy mixture.

4 Heat oil in wok or large frying pan; stir-fry ribs, in batches, until browned all over.

5 Add remaining ingredients to wok; cook, stirring, until sugar dissolves. Return ribs to wok; stir-fry until heated through.

SERVES 4

per serving 17.7g fat; 2066kJ

tip Spicy spare ribs can be made a day ahead and kept, covered, in the refrigerator or, if desired, frozen for up to 3 months. To serve, reheat in the microwave oven or wok.

serving suggestion Serve with steamed rice, and individual finger bowls filled with water and a few slices of lemon.

indonesian beef satay

PREPARATION TIME 15 MINUTES • COOKING TIME 25 MINUTES

Satays are one of the most popular dishes throughout South-East Asia and are the number-one street food in Indonesian cities. They're equally good served on a plate with sticky rice.

1 teaspoon peanut oil

1 small brown onion (80g), chopped finely

2 cloves garlic, crushed

2 red thai chillies, seeded, chopped finely

1/4 teaspoon shrimp paste

1/2 cup (140g) crunchy peanut butter

1 tablespoon brown sugar

1 teaspoon light soy sauce

1/2 cup (125ml) coconut cream

750g beef rump steak, chopped coarsely

1/4 cup (60ml) beef stock

1 Heat oil in medium saucepan; cook onion, garlic and chilli, stirring, until onion softens. Add paste, peanut butter, sugar and sauce. Gradually stir in coconut cream; bring to a boil. Reduce heat; simmer, uncovered, about 1 minute or until sauce thickens slightly. Cool 5 minutes.

2 Combine beef with half of the peanut sauce in large bowl; thread beef onto 12 bamboo skewers.

3 Cook skewers on heated oiled grill plate (or grill or barbecue) until beef is browned all over and cooked as desired.

4 Meanwhile, add stock to remaining peanut sauce; cook, stirring, over low heat, until heated through.

5 Serve satay skewers with remaining peanut sauce.

SERVES 4

per serving 34g fat; 2282kJ

tips Soak 12 bamboo skewers in water while preparing the ingredients to prevent them scorching and splintering during cooking.

You can substitute chicken, pork or lamb for the beef, if you prefer.

serving suggestion Serve with boiled white rice and a plate of refreshing cucumber slices.

jungle pork stir-fry

PREPARATION TIME 15 MINUTES • COOKING TIME 15 MINUTES

This recipe is a variation of Thai jungle pork curry – rated one of the hottest!

1 tablespoon peanut oil
1kg pork fillets, sliced thinly
1 medium brown onion (150g),
**   sliced thinly**
2 red thai chillies, sliced thinly
1 tablespoon finely chopped
**   lemon grass**
1 tablespoon drained, coarsely
**   chopped green peppercorns**
1 tablespoon finely chopped
**   palm sugar**
1 tablespoon finely grated
**   fresh galangal**
4 fresh kaffir lime leaves,
**   shredded finely**
2 tablespoons green curry paste
100g thai eggplants, halved
1 cup (250ml) coconut cream
¼ cup loosely packed fresh thai
**   basil leaves**

1 Heat oil in wok or large frying pan; stir-fry pork and onion, in batches, until pork is browned all over.

2 Add chilli, lemon grass, peppercorns, sugar, galangal, lime leaves and paste to wok; stir-fry until fragrant.

3 Return pork mixture to wok with eggplant and cream; stir-fry until eggplant is just tender. Stir in basil.

SERVES 4

per serving 27g fat; 2136kJ

tip Galangal is a dried root with a piquant peppery flavour. You can substitute fresh ginger for the galangal, if unavailable.

serving suggestion Serve with boiled or steamed white long-grain rice.

lamb and spinach curry

PREPARATION TIME 15 MINUTES • COOKING TIME 25 MINUTES

*This recipe, called saag gosht in India, is one of our favourites. You can use fresh spinach leaves
if you like, but they need to be softened in boiling water then processed before using.*

2 tablespoons vegetable oil
750g lamb fillets, sliced thinly
2 medium brown onions (300g),
  chopped finely
3 cloves garlic, crushed
2 teaspoons grated fresh ginger
1 teaspoon chilli powder
1 cinnamon stick
5 whole cloves
5 cardamom pods, bruised
2 teaspoons ground coriander
2 teaspoons ground cumin
1/2 teaspoon ground turmeric
1 tablespoon garam masala
2 teaspoons black mustard seeds
2 tablespoons tomato paste
600ml buttermilk
1/2 cup (120g) sour cream
600g frozen spinach,
  thawed, drained

1 Heat half of the oil in large saucepan; cook lamb, in batches, until browned all over.

2 Heat remaining oil in same pan; cook onion, garlic and ginger, stirring, until onion softens. Add spices and paste; cook, stirring, until fragrant.

3 Return lamb to pan with remaining ingredients; bring to a boil. Reduce heat; simmer, uncovered, about 15 minutes or until sauce thickens.

SERVES 4

per serving 32.6g fat; 2417kJ

tip Use your hands to squeeze out as much excess water from the spinach as possible.

serving suggestion Serve with steamed basmati rice, cucumber raita and warm naan.

pork vindaloo

PREPARATION TIME 10 MINUTES • COOKING TIME 25 MINUTES

*Hot and spicy vindaloo is a speciality of Goa, the once-Portuguese state on the west coast of India.
While you can make your own vindaloo paste, commercial versions are adequate substitutes.*

750g pork fillets
1 tablespoon vegetable oil
2 large brown onions (400g),
  sliced thinly
1/2 cup (150g) vindaloo
  curry paste
2 medium red capsicums (400g),
  sliced thinly
1 tablespoon cornflour
1 cup (250ml) water
1/3 cup (80ml) lime juice
2 green onions, sliced thinly

1 Cut pork into 2.5cm pieces.

2 Heat oil in large saucepan; cook brown onion, stirring, until just soft. Add pork, paste and capsicum; cook, stirring, about 5 minutes or until pork is changed in colour and cooked through.

3 Stir in blended cornflour and water; cook, stirring, until mixture boils and thickens. Reduce heat; simmer, uncovered, about 20 minutes or until pork is tender. Remove from heat; stir in juice and green onion.

SERVES 4

per serving 20.9g fat; 1828kJ

tip Like many curries, the flavours in this vindaloo are enhanced if made a day ahead and refrigerated, covered. You can also freeze this curry for up to three months.

serving suggestion Serve with steamed basmati rice and cucumber raita.

pork-filled bean-curd pouches

PREPARATION TIME 30 MINUTES • COOKING TIME 10 MINUTES

Seasoned fried bean-curd skins are available from most Japanese grocery stores. Koshihikari rice is available from all major supermarkets but medium- or short-grain rice can be substituted.

¹/₂ cup (100g) koshihikari rice
2 teaspoons peanut oil
2 green onions, sliced thinly
1 clove garlic, crushed
¹/₂ teaspoon grated fresh ginger
2 red thai chillies, seeded, chopped finely
350g pork mince
12 seasoned fried bean-curd skins
12 chives

SESAME-LIME DIPPING SAUCE
¹/₄ cup (60ml) light soy sauce
2 tablespoons seasoned rice vinegar
1 teaspoon sugar
1 tablespoon lime juice
2 drops sesame oil

Cut open bean-curd skin and gently push fingers into corners to form pouch

Push pork mixture into corners of pouch then secure with a chive

1 Cook rice in large saucepan of boiling water, uncovered, until just tender; drain.

2 Meanwhile, heat oil in medium frying pan; cook onion, garlic, ginger and chilli until onion softens. Add pork; cook, stirring, until changed in colour and cooked through. Add rice to pork mixture; toss to combine.

3 Carefully cut open a bean-curd skin on one side, gently pushing fingers into each corner to form pouch. Fill pouch with a twelfth of the pork mixture, pushing mixture into corners but being careful not to overfill or tear pouch. Tie pouch with a chive to enclose filling. Repeat with remaining pork mixture, bean-curd skins and chives. Serve pouches with sesame-lime dipping sauce.

sesame-lime dipping sauce Combine ingredients in small bowl.

SERVES 4

per serving 13.1g fat; 1345kJ

tip You can substitute green onions for the chives if you prefer.

serving suggestion This could be a substantial starter before a main course of hoisin vegetable stir-fry (see page 46).

sweet and sour pork

PREPARATION TIME 15 MINUTES • COOKING TIME 15 MINUTES

Sweet and sour are two flavours considered essential to a well-balanced meal by the Chinese, but combining the two in one dish is thought to have been an attempt to cater to the European palate.

750g pork fillets
¹/₄ cup (35g) cornflour
440g can pineapple pieces in
  natural juice
vegetable oil, for deep-frying
1 tablespoon peanut oil
1 medium brown onion (150g),
  sliced thickly
1 medium red capsicum (200g),
  chopped coarsely
1 medium green capsicum (200g),
  chopped coarsely
1 trimmed stick celery (75g),
  chopped coarsely
2 tablespoons tomato sauce
2 tablespoons plum sauce
2 tablespoons light soy sauce
¹/₄ cup (60ml) white vinegar
1 tablespoon cornflour, extra
¹/₄ cup (60ml) chicken stock

1　Slice pork into 1cm-thick slices. Coat pork in cornflour; shake off excess.

2　Drain pineapple over small bowl; reserve juice and pineapple separately.

3　Heat vegetable oil in medium frying pan; deep-fry pork, in batches, until browned all over. Drain on absorbent paper.

4　Heat peanut oil in wok or large frying pan; stir-fry onion until just soft. Add capsicums and celery; stir-fry until vegetables are just tender.

5　Stir in combined sauces, vinegar, and extra cornflour blended with stock and reserved juice; cook, stirring, until mixture boils and thickens.

6　Add pork and pineapple; stir-fry until heated through.

SERVES 4

per serving　19.5g fat; 1986kJ

tip　Placing pork, wrapped in plastic wrap, in the freezer for about 1 hour makes it easier to slice.

serving suggestion　Serve with steamed white long-grain rice and crisp prawn crackers.

balinese-style lamb

PREPARATION TIME 15 MINUTES • COOKING TIME 15 MINUTES

Kecap manis – a sweet, thick, Indonesian soy sauce – is available from all Asian grocery stores and most large supermarkets. Shrimp paste is often sold as trasi or blachan in Asian food stores... use it sparingly because a little goes a long way! You will need a piece of ginger about 5cm long for this recipe.

5 red thai chillies, seeded, chopped coarsely

1/2 teaspoon shrimp paste

2 medium brown onions (300g), chopped coarsely

3 cloves garlic, quartered

50g fresh ginger, peeled, chopped coarsely

2 tablespoons desiccated coconut, toasted

1 tablespoon peanut oil

1kg lamb fillets, sliced thinly

1 tablespoon coarsely grated palm sugar

1 tablespoon kecap manis

1 tablespoon dark soy sauce

1 tablespoon lime juice

1 Blend or process chilli, paste, onion, garlic, ginger and coconut until mixture forms a paste.

2 Heat oil in wok or large frying pan; stir-fry lamb, in batches, until browned all over. Add chilli mixture to wok; stir-fry until fragrant.

3 Return lamb to wok with combined remaining ingredients; stir-fry until heated through.

SERVES 4

per serving 15.8g fat; 1646kJ

tip Brown or black sugar can be used as a substitute for palm sugar.

serving suggestion Serve with steamed jasmine rice and stir-fried snow peas.

tandoori lamb cutlets

PREPARATION TIME 20 MINUTES • COOKING TIME 10 MINUTES

Ready-made tandoori paste gives food the traditional red-orange hue it gets when cooked in a tandoor, a round-top brick and clay oven the Indians use to smoke, bake or roast a great many different foods.

12 lamb cutlets (900g)
1/2 cup (150g) tandoori paste
3/4 cup (210g) yogurt

CHUTNEY
1 tablespoon vegetable oil
1 small red onion (100g), chopped finely
2 large tomatoes (500g), chopped finely
1 tablespoon lime juice
1 tablespoon sweet chilli sauce
2 tablespoons finely chopped fresh coriander

RAITA
1 lebanese cucumber (130g), seeded, chopped finely
2 tablespoons finely chopped fresh mint
3/4 cup (210g) yogurt

1 Combine lamb with paste and yogurt in large bowl.

2 Heat oil in large non-stick frying pan; cook lamb, in batches, until browned both sides and cooked as desired.

3 Serve lamb with separate bowls of chutney and raita.

chutney Combine ingredients in small bowl.

raita Combine ingredients in small bowl.

SERVES 4

per serving 49.4g fat; 2553kJ

tip Lamb can be marinated a day ahead and refrigerated, covered.

serving suggestion Serve with naan, sprinkled with black cumin seeds and warmed in the oven.

stir-fried sukiyaki

PREPARATION TIME 15 MINUTES • COOKING TIME 20 MINUTES

This recipe is a variation of the traditional Japanese version, which is cooked at the table and served in individual portions. You will need about half a small chinese cabbage to make this recipe.

300g firm tofu
1 tablespoon peanut oil
500g beef rump steak,
   sliced thinly
4 green onions, chopped coarsely
225g can sliced water
   chestnuts, drained
1 large carrot (180g),
   sliced thinly
2 trimmed sticks celery (150g),
   sliced thickly
100g fresh shiitake mushrooms,
   sliced thinly
2¹/₂ cups (175g) coarsely
   shredded chinese cabbage
¹/₄ cup (60ml) light soy sauce
¹/₂ cup (125ml) beef stock
1 tablespoon brown sugar

1 Cut tofu into 3cm cubes.

2 Heat half of the oil in wok or large frying pan; stir-fry beef, in batches, until browned all over.

3 Heat remaining oil in wok; stir-fry onion and water chestnuts until onion softens. Add carrot, celery and mushrooms; stir-fry until just tender.

4 Return beef to wok with remaining ingredients; stir-fry until cabbage just wilts.

SERVES 4

per serving 16.1g fat; 1465kJ

tip Very thinly sliced beef, sold as yaki-niku or sukiyaki beef, is available from Asian grocery stores. You can substitute beef sirloin or rib eye (scotch fillet) if you prefer.

serving suggestion The traditional noodles to serve with sukiyaki are the fresh gelatinous variety known as shirataki, but you can substitute cooked cellophane, harusame or even rice stick noodles if you prefer.

cantonese beef stir-fry

PREPARATION TIME 20 MINUTES • COOKING TIME 20 MINUTES

Texture is an important component of Cantonese cooking, and this dish, with its varying textures and delicate flavours, is typical of this region's cuisine.

600g fresh rice noodles
2 tablespoons peanut oil
750g beef fillet, sliced thinly
1 teaspoon finely grated
    orange rind
1 tablespoon grated fresh ginger
2 cloves garlic, crushed
2 cups (170g) broccoli florets
1 large red capsicum (350g),
    chopped coarsely
1 tablespoon cornflour
1/2 cup (125ml) beef stock
10 fresh shiitake mushrooms,
    sliced thinly
1/2 cup (125ml) light soy sauce
1/3 cup (80ml) plum sauce
1 tablespoon brown sugar
3 cups (210g) coarsely
    shredded cabbage

1 Rinse noodles under hot running water; drain. Transfer to large bowl; separate noodles with fork.

2 Heat half of the oil in wok or large frying pan; stir-fry beef, in batches, until browned all over.

3 Heat remaining oil in wok; cook rind, ginger and garlic, stirring, until fragrant. Add broccoli and capsicum; cook, stirring, until just tender.

4 Blend cornflour and stock in small bowl; add to wok with beef, mushrooms, combined sauces and sugar. Bring to a boil; reduce heat. Cook, stirring, until sauce thickens slightly. Add noodles and cabbage; cook, stirring, until cabbage just wilts.

SERVES 4

per serving 19.9g fat; 3064kJ

tip Don't have fresh rice noodles? Then substitute hokkien or fresh wheat noodles instead – but be sure to check the manufacturer's instructions regarding their preparation.

serving suggestion This hearty dish could be livened up with a little chilli; place it in a separate bowl so that guests can have as much, or as little, as they like.

sang choy bow

PREPARATION TIME 15 MINUTES • COOKING TIME 15 MINUTES

Packages of already-fried wheat noodles are available from major supermarkets in both spaghetti- and fettuccine-widths – we used the thinner variety here.

1 tablespoon peanut oil
750g pork mince
2 cloves garlic, crushed
225g can water chestnuts,
    drained, chopped finely
1 teaspoon sambal oelek
1 tablespoon lime juice
1 medium red capsicum (200g),
    chopped finely
1 trimmed stick celery (75g),
    chopped finely
2 tablespoons light soy sauce
2 tablespoons rice vinegar
100g packet fried crunchy noodles
8 large iceberg lettuce leaves
2 green onions, sliced thinly

1 Heat oil in wok or large frying pan; stir-fry pork and garlic about 5 minutes or until pork changes colour and is cooked through.

2 Stir in water chestnuts, sambal, juice, capsicum, celery, sauce and vinegar; cook, stirring, until vegetables are just tender. Remove from heat; stir in noodles.

3 Place two lettuce leaves on each serving plate. Divide pork mixture among leaves; sprinkle each with onion.

SERVES 4

per serving 21.3g fat; 1695kJ

tip The pork mixture, without the noodles, can be made a day ahead and refrigerated, covered. Add noodles just before serving so they retain their crunch.

serving suggestion Serve with vegetarian rice-paper rolls or steamed dim sum.

korean-style barbecued cutlets

PREPARATION TIME 15 MINUTES • COOKING TIME 5 MINUTES

This recipe is an adaptation of the famous Korean barbecued dish bulgogi, where strips of beef are coated in a spicy mixture and barbecued over glowing coals. Today, a variety of meats – including chicken, pork and lamb – are cooked in this manner.

1/2 cup (125ml) light soy sauce
1 cup (250ml) mirin
2 green onions, sliced thinly
2 cloves garlic, crushed
1 tablespoon grated fresh ginger
1 tablespoon brown sugar
1 tablespoon cracked
    black pepper
1 tablespoon plain flour
16 lamb cutlets (1kg), trimmed

1 Combine sauce, mirin, onion, garlic, ginger, sugar, pepper and flour in large bowl. Add cutlets; toss to coat all over in spice mixture.

2 Cook drained cutlets on heated oiled grill plate (or grill or barbecue) until browned both sides and cooked as desired. Brush occasionally with marinade during cooking.

SERVES 4

per serving 11.7g fat; 1370kJ

tip Cutlets can be marinated a day ahead and refrigerated, covered. Traditionally, bulgogi beef was marinated overnight to intensify the flavour.

serving suggestion Serve with steamed jasmine rice and Asian greens, like bok choy, snake beans or snow peas.

beef rendang

PREPARATION TIME 15 MINUTES • COOKING TIME 15 MINUTES

This famous Sumatran dish is usually simmered for long periods, in rich spices and coconut milk, until the meat is tender and almost dry. We've adjusted the recipe somewhat so you can make it in less than 30 minutes! You will need a piece of ginger about 2cm long to make this recipe.

2 medium brown onions (300g)
2 cloves garlic, quartered
20g piece fresh ginger, peeled
1 tablespoon coarsely chopped
    lemon grass
1 tablespoon peanut oil
1kg beef fillet, sliced thinly
1 cinnamon stick
2 whole cloves
1 tablespoon ground coriander
1 tablespoon ground cumin
1/2 cup (45g) desiccated coconut
1 tablespoon tamarind concentrate
1/4 cup (60ml) coconut cream

1 Blend or process one quartered onion, garlic, ginger and lemon grass until mixture is almost smooth. Finely chop remaining onion.

2 Heat oil in wok or large frying pan; stir-fry beef and remaining onion, in batches, until beef is browned all over.

3 Add onion mixture to wok with spices and coconut; stir-fry until fragrant.

4 Return beef mixture to wok with tamarind and coconut cream; stir-fry until rendang is almost dry.

SERVES 4

per serving 27.9g fat; 2132kJ

tips You can substitute chicken or duck for the beef, if you prefer.
This recipe can be made a day ahead and refrigerated, covered.

serving suggestion Beef rendang is traditionally eaten with sticky rice cooked in coconut milk, but steamed or boiled rice is just as good.

warm chilli beef salad

PREPARATION TIME 15 MINUTES • COOKING TIME 15 MINUTES

The salad ingredients in this Thai speciality are cooked just long enough to warm them through.
You will need half a medium chinese cabbage to make this recipe.

2 tablespoons peanut oil
750g beef fillets, sliced thinly
1 medium white onion (150g),
  sliced thinly
2 red thai chillies, seeded,
  chopped finely
3 cloves garlic, crushed
2 tablespoons light soy sauce
1 teaspoon fish sauce
1 tablespoon sweet chilli sauce
2 tablespoons lime juice
250g cherry tomatoes, halved
3 cups (210g) finely shredded
  chinese cabbage
3/4 cup loosely packed fresh
  mint leaves
1 medium green cucumber (170g),
  seeded, sliced thinly
1 cup (80g) bean sprouts

1 Heat half of the oil in wok or large frying pan; stir-fry beef, in batches, until browned all over.

2 Heat remaining oil in wok; stir-fry onion, chilli and garlic until onion softens.

3 Return beef to wok with combined sauces, juice, tomato and cabbage; stir-fry until cabbage just wilts.

4 Place beef mixture in large serving bowl. Stir in mint, cucumber and sprouts; serve immediately.

SERVES 4

per serving 18.7g fat; 1554kJ

tip Place beef in freezer, in plastic wrap, for about 1 hour before use to make it easier to slice.

serving suggestion Serve with a bowl of sambal oelek, the fiery-hot Indonesian chilli and vinegar condiment.

beef donburi

PREPARATION TIME 15 MINUTES • COOKING TIME 10 MINUTES

Donburi refers to a certain size of rice bowl, usually with a lid, and also the meat or poultry/rice combination which is served in it. Koshihikari rice is grown from Japanese seed; substitute medium-grain white rice if desired.

1 cup (200g) koshihikari rice
500g beef rump steak,
** sliced thinly**
1 clove garlic, crushed
1 teaspoon grated fresh ginger
1/2 cup (125ml) light soy sauce
1/2 cup (125ml) mirin
1 tablespoon peanut oil
6 green onions, sliced thinly

1 Cook rice in large saucepan of boiling water, uncovered, until just tender; drain.

2 Meanwhile, combine beef, garlic and ginger in medium bowl with half of the soy sauce and half of the mirin.

3 Heat oil in large frying pan; cook beef, in batches, stirring, until browned all over. Return beef to pan with remaining soy sauce and mirin; bring to a boil.

4 Serve beef mixture over rice in large soup or rice bowls; sprinkle with onion.

SERVES 4

per serving 10.6g fat; 1794kJ

tip You can use thinly sliced chicken breast fillets rather than beef in this recipe; if you do, thinly slice a large brown onion and add it to the chicken mixture before cooking.

serving suggestion Serve with vegetable tempura.

peanut beef curry

PREPARATION TIME 20 MINUTES • COOKING TIME 15 MINUTES

This hot and spicy curry combines the best of two countries – the fragrant spices of Indian cooking and the coconut-and-citrus flavours of the Thai kitchen. While we've chosen snow peas as the vegetable component, you can use any vegetable you have on hand – even potatoes.

1 tablespoon vegetable oil
750g beef fillet, sliced thinly
1¹/₄ cups (310ml) coconut milk
¹/₂ cup (75g) roasted peanuts
1 tablespoon brown sugar
1 tablespoon cornflour
¹/₃ cup (80ml) lime juice
250g snow peas

CURRY PASTE
2 tablespoons vegetable oil
5 cloves garlic, crushed
1 tablespoon grated fresh ginger
4 green onions, chopped coarsely
1 tablespoon coarsely chopped lemon grass
1 tablespoon dried chilli flakes
1 teaspoon ground cumin
1 tablespoon ground coriander
1 teaspoon shrimp paste
1 cup (250ml) coconut milk

1 Heat oil in wok or large frying pan; stir-fry beef, in batches, until browned all over.

2 Return beef to wok with coconut milk, peanuts, sugar and curry paste; bring to a boil. Reduce heat; simmer, uncovered, about 10 minutes or until beef is tender.

3 Add blended cornflour and juice; bring to a boil. Reduce heat; simmer, uncovered, until sauce thickens.

4 Add snow peas; toss gently to combine.

curry paste Heat oil in medium saucepan; cook garlic, ginger, onion, lemon grass, spices and paste, stirring, until fragrant. Blend or process garlic mixture with coconut milk until smooth.

SERVES 4

per serving 61.6g fat; 3435kJ

tip Preparing a large quantity of curry paste in a food processor makes blending much easier and smoother; however, if you intend to keep the paste for future use, leave out the coconut milk. Place curry paste in a jar, seal it tightly, and refrigerate for up to four months.

serving suggestion The ideal accompaniment to this curry is a large platter of steamed or boiled jasmine rice and a bowl of minted yogurt.

fried beef and carrots

PREPARATION TIME 15 MINUTES • COOKING TIME 25 MINUTES

This recipe is a variation of the northern Chinese recipe, twice-fried shredded beef. We have only fried our beef once but, if you wish to spend the extra time, it's even yummier if fried twice.

**750g beef rump steak,
    sliced thinly**
1/4 cup (60ml) light soy sauce
2 tablespoons hoisin sauce
2 tablespoons rice vinegar
1/4 cup (35g) cornflour
vegetable oil, for deep-frying
3 medium carrots (360g)
4 green onions, sliced thinly
2 red thai chillies, sliced thinly
1 clove garlic, crushed

1 Combine beef with 1 tablespoon each of sauces and vinegar in medium bowl. Coat beef, in batches, in cornflour; shake off excess.

2 Heat oil in wok or large saucepan; deep-fry beef, in batches, until browned all over. Drain on absorbent paper.

3 Cut carrots into matchstick-sized pieces. Deep-fry carrot, in batches, until tender; drain on absorbent paper.

4 Combine beef with carrot, onion and chilli in large bowl. Add combined remaining sauces, remaining vinegar and garlic; toss gently.

SERVES 4

per serving 25g fat; 1937kJ

tips You can purchase beef strips from your butcher to reduce the time it takes to slice the beef.

For a milder version of this recipe, remove seeds from the chillies.

serving suggestion Serve with steamed or boiled jasmine rice, and small bowls of light soy sauce and chilli sauce.

beef tataki

PREPARATION TIME 15 MINUTES • COOKING TIME 10 MINUTES

This Japanese dish requires very fresh beef fillet to be quickly seared over a high flame or hot coals
so the scorched exterior contrasts dramatically with the raw red centre. Dried bonito flakes
are available from Asian grocery stores. You need a small cabbage to make this recipe.

500g piece beef rump, trimmed
1 tablespoon vegetable oil
5 cups (350g) finely
 shredded cabbage
4 green onions, sliced thinly
2 tablespoons pink pickled ginger
8 mint leaves
2 teaspoons wasabi

SOY DIPPING SAUCE
¹/₃ cup (80ml) lemon juice
¹/₃ cup (80ml) light soy sauce
2 tablespoons sake
1 tablespoon mirin
2 tablespoons bonito flakes
1 teaspoon sugar

1 Cook beef on heated oiled grill plate (or grill or barbecue) about
 10 minutes or until browned all over. Place beef in large bowl of cold
 water to halt cooking process; cool.

2 Meanwhile, heat oil in large frying pan; cook cabbage and 1 tablespoon
 of the soy dipping sauce, stirring, until just wilted.

3 Slice beef thinly; serve on cabbage with onion, ginger, mint, wasabi
 and individual bowls of remaining soy dipping sauce.

soy dipping sauce Combine ingredients in small saucepan; cook,
stirring, until sugar dissolves. Cool then strain over small bowl;
discard solids.

SERVES 4

per serving 15.6g fat; 1246kJ

tip You can substitute beef fillet, rib eye (scotch fillet) or sirloin
steak for the rump if desired. If you are unable to buy sake, you can
substitute rice vinegar instead.

serving suggestion Serve with steamed or boiled short-grain white rice.

thai beef salad

PREPARATION TIME 15 MINUTES (plus standing time)
COOKING TIME 15 MINUTES

This dish, known in Thailand as yum nua, often has the major ingredients arranged separately on a platter; here, we've tossed them all together.

500g beef fillet
3 medium green cucumbers (510g),
    peeled, sliced thickly
4 red thai chillies, sliced thinly
3 green onions, sliced thinly
1/2 cup loosely packed
    fresh mint leaves
1/2 cup loosely packed
    fresh coriander leaves

LEMON GRASS DRESSING
1 clove garlic, crushed
2 teaspoons finely chopped
    lemon grass
2 teaspoons finely chopped
    fresh coriander root
1 tablespoon lime juice
2 tablespoons light soy sauce
1/2 teaspoon fish sauce
2 teaspoons brown sugar

1 Cook beef on heated oiled grill plate (or grill or barbecue) until browned all over and cooked as desired. Stand 5 minutes; slice thinly.

2 Place beef, cucumber, chilli, onion, herbs and lemon grass dressing in large bowl; toss gently to combine.

lemon grass dressing Combine ingredients in small bowl.

SERVES 4

per serving 6.3g fat; 792kJ

tip If you're running short on time, you can substitute thin slices of rare roast beef for the beef fillet.

serving suggestion Serve with deep-fried crispy rice noodles, also known as mee krob or mee grob, for an authentic Thai experience.

glossary

baby new potato also known as chats; not a particular type of potato, but simply an early harvest.

beans, green sometimes called french beans.

broccolini milder and sweeter than the traditional broccoli, it is completely edible from flower to stem and has a delicate flavour with a subtle, peppery edge. This versatile vegetable is a cross between broccoli and chinese kale, and is sometimes known as baby broccoli; has a long, slender stem and is topped with small flowering buds.

butter use salted or unsalted ("sweet") butter; 125g is equal to one stick of butter.

buttermilk (1.8g fat per 100ml) sold alongside fresh milk products in supermarkets; despite the implication of its name, is low in fat. Originally the liquid left after butter was churned, today, it is commercially made similarly to yogurt. A good lower-fat substitution for dairy products such as cream or sour cream; good in baking and in salad dressings.

capsicum also known as bell pepper or, simply, pepper. Seeds and membranes should be discarded before use.

cayenne pepper a thin-fleshed, long, extremely hot red chilli; usually purchased dried and ground.

chicken

BREAST FILLET breast halved, skinned and boned.

LOVELY LEG also known as a drummette; skinless drumstick with the end of the bone removed.

MINCE finely ground fresh chicken.

THIGH FILLET thigh skinned and boned.

chives related to the onion and leek, with subtle onion flavour. Chives and flowering chives are interchangeable.

cornflour also known as cornstarch; used as a thickening agent in cooking.

creamed corn available in various-sized cans from most supermarkets.

cucumber we used large green cucumbers in this book unless otherwise specified.

LEBANESE long, slender and thin-skinned; this variety also known as the european or burpless cucumber.

eggplant also known as aubergine.

fennel also known as finocchio or anise; eaten raw in salads or braised or fried as a vegetable accompaniment. Also the name given to dried seeds having a licorice flavour.

green peppercorns soft, unripe berry of the pepper plant usually sold in brine, having a distinctive and fresh taste.

lamb

FILLET tenderloin; the smaller piece of meat from a row of loin chops or cutlets.

FRENCH-TRIMMED CUTLET all the fat and gristle at the narrow end of the bone is discarded then the remaining meat trimmed.

MINCE also known as ground lamb.

mesclun is a salad mix or gourmet salad mix with a mixture of assorted young lettuce and other green leaves, including baby spinach leaves, mizuna and curly endive.

muslin plain, finely woven cotton fabric. Often used to strain stocks and sauces. If unavailable, use disposable coffee filter papers.

nuts

CASHEW we used unsalted roasted cashews in this book. They are available from health food stores and most supermarkets.

MACADAMIA native to Australia, rich and buttery nut; store in refrigerator because of high oil content.

oil

COOKING-OIL SPRAY vegetable oil in an aerosol can; available in supermarkets.

OLIVE mono-unsaturated; made from the pressing of tree-ripened olives. Extra virgin and virgin are the highest quality olive oils, obtained from the first pressings of the olives. Extra light or light describes the milder flavours, not the fat levels.

VEGETABLE any of a number of oils sourced from plants rather than animal fats.

onion

GREEN also known as scallion or (incorrectly) shallot; an immature onion picked before the bulb has formed, having a long, bright-green edible stalk.

RED also known as spanish, red spanish or bermuda onion; a sweet-flavoured, large purple-red onion.

SPRING have crisp, narrow green-leafed tops and a smallish round sweet white bulb.

paprika ground dried red capsicum (bell pepper); available sweet or hot.

plum sauce a thick, sweet and sour dipping sauce made from plums, vinegar, sugar, chillies and spices.

pork

BUTTERFLY skinless, boneless mid-loin chop, split in half and flattened.

FILLET skinless, boneless eye-fillet cut from the loin.

MINCE finely ground fresh pork.

SPARE RIBS cut from the pork belly.

prawns also known as shrimp.

pulses

LENTILS (red, brown, yellow) dried pulses often identified by and named after their colour; also known as dhal.

quail small, delicate-flavoured, domestically grown game birds ranging in weight from 250g to 300g; also known as partridge.

rice

BASMATI a fragrant, long-grained white rice. It should be washed several times before cooking.

KOSHIHIKARI small, round-grain white rice. Substitute short-grain white rice and cook by the absorption method.

LONG-GRAIN elongated grains, stay separate when cooked.

WHITE is hulled and polished, can be short- or long-grained.

scallops a bivalve mollusc with fluted shell valve; we used scallops having the coral (roe) attached.

snow peas also known as mange tout ("eat all"). Snow pea tendrils, the growing shoots of the plant, are sold by green grocers.

squid hoods convenient cleaned squid (calamari).

stock 1 cup (250ml) stock is the equivalent of 1 cup (250ml) water plus 1 crumbled stock cube (or 1 teaspoon stock powder). If you prefer to make your own fresh stock, see recipes on page 118.

sugar we used coarse granulated table sugar, also known as crystal sugar, unless otherwise specified.

water chestnuts resemble chestnuts in appearance, hence the English name. They are small brown tubes with a crisp, white, nutty-tasting flesh. Their crunchy texture is best experienced fresh, however, canned water chestnuts are more easily obtained and can be refrigerated for about a month after opening.

yogurt plain, unflavoured yogurt – in addition to being good eaten on its own – can be used as a meat tenderiser, as the basis for various sauces and dips or as an enricher and thickener.

zucchini also known as courgette; green or grey member of the squash family having edible flowers.

index

make your own stock

These recipes can be made up to 4 days ahead and refrigerated, covered. Be sure to remove any fat from the surface after the cooled stock has been refrigerated overnight. If the stock is to be kept longer, it is best to freeze it in smaller quantities. *All stock recipes make about 2.5 litres (10 cups).*

Stock is also available in cans or tetra packs. Stock cubes or powder can be used. As a guide, 1 teaspoon of stock powder or 1 small crumbled stock cube mixed with 1 cup (250ml) water will give a fairly strong stock. Be aware of the salt and fat content of stock cubes and powders and prepared stocks.

BEEF STOCK

2kg meaty beef bones
2 medium onions (300g)
2 trimmed sticks celery (150g), chopped coarsely
2 medium carrots (250g), chopped coarsely
3 bay leaves
2 teaspoons black peppercorns
5 litres (20 cups) water
3 litres (12 cups) water, extra

Place bones and unpeeled chopped onions in baking dish. Bake in hot oven about 1 hour or until bones and onions are well browned. Transfer bones and onions to large saucepan; add celery, carrots, bay leaves, peppercorns and water. Simmer, uncovered, 3 hours; add extra water. Simmer, uncovered, further 1 hour; strain.

CHICKEN STOCK

2kg chicken bones
2 medium onions (300g), chopped coarsely
2 trimmed sticks celery (150g), chopped coarsely
2 medium carrots (250g), chopped coarsely
3 bay leaves
2 teaspoons black peppercorns
5 litres (20 cups) water

Combine ingredients in large saucepan. Simmer, uncovered, 2 hours; strain.

FISH STOCK

1.5kg fish bones
3 litres (12 cups) water
1 medium onion (150g), chopped coarsely
2 trimmed sticks celery (150g), chopped coarsely
2 bay leaves
1 teaspoon black peppercorns

Combine ingredients in large saucepan. Simmer, uncovered, 20 minutes; strain.

VEGETABLE STOCK

2 large carrots (360g), chopped coarsely
2 large parsnips (360g), chopped coarsely
4 medium onions (600g), chopped coarsely
12 trimmed sticks celery (900g), chopped coarsely
4 bay leaves
2 teaspoons black peppercorns
6 litres (24 cups) water

Combine ingredients in large saucepan. Simmer, uncovered, 1¹/2 hours; strain.

facts and figures

Wherever you live, you'll be able to use our recipes with the help of these easy-to-follow conversions. While these conversions are approximate only, the difference between an exact and the approximate conversion of various liquid and dry measures is but minimal and will not affect your cooking results.

dry measures

metric	imperial
15g	1/2oz
30g	1oz
60g	2oz
90g	3oz
125g	4oz (1/4lb)
155g	5oz
185g	6oz
220g	7oz
250g	8oz (1/2lb)
280g	9oz
315g	10oz
345g	11oz
375g	12oz (3/4lb)
410g	13oz
440g	14oz
470g	15oz
500g	16oz (1lb)
750g	24oz (11/2lb)
1kg	32oz (2lb)

oven temperatures

These oven temperatures are only a guide. Always check the manufacturer's manual.

	°C (Celsius)	°F (Fahrenheit)	Gas Mark
Very slow	120	250	1
Slow	150	300	2
Moderately slow	160	325	3
Moderate	180 - 190	350 - 375	4
Moderately hot	200 - 210	400 - 425	5
Hot	220 - 230	450 - 475	6
Very hot	240 - 250	500 - 525	7

liquid measures

metric	imperial
30ml	1 fluid oz
60ml	2 fluid oz
100ml	3 fluid oz
125ml	4 fluid oz
150ml	5 fluid oz (1/4 pint/1 gill)
190ml	6 fluid oz
250ml	8 fluid oz
300ml	10 fluid oz (1/2 pint)
500ml	16 fluid oz
600ml	20 fluid oz (1 pint)
1000ml (1 litre)	13/4 pints

helpful measures

metric	imperial
3mm	1/8in
6mm	1/4in
1cm	1/2in
2cm	3/4in
2.5cm	1in
5cm	2in
6cm	21/2in
8cm	3in
10cm	4in
13cm	5in
15cm	6in
18cm	7in
20cm	8in
23cm	9in
25cm	10in
28cm	11in
30cm	12in (1ft)

helpful measures

The difference between one country's measuring cups and another's is, at most, within a 2 or 3 teaspoon variance. (For the record, 1 Australian metric measuring cup holds approximately 250ml.) The most accurate way of measuring dry ingredients is to weigh them. When measuring liquids, use a clear glass or plastic jug with the metric markings. (One Australian metric tablespoon holds 20ml; one Australian metric teaspoon holds 5ml.)

If you would like to purchase *The Australian Women's Weekly* Test Kitchen's metric measuring cups and spoons (as approved by Standards Australia), turn to page 120 for details and order coupon. You will receive:

- a graduated set of 4 cups for measuring dry ingredients, with sizes marked on the cups.
- a graduated set of 4 spoons for measuring dry and liquid ingredients, with amounts marked on the spoons.

Note: North America, NZ and the UK use 15ml tablespoons. All cup and spoon measurements are level.

We use large eggs having an average weight of 60g.

how to measure

When using graduated metric measuring cups, shake dry ingredients loosely into the appropriate cup. Do not tap the cup on a bench or tightly pack the ingredients unless directed to do so. Level top of measuring cups and measuring spoons with a knife. When measuring liquids, place a clear glass or plastic jug with metric markings on a flat surface to check accuracy at eye level.

Looking after **your interest...**

Keep your Home Library cookbooks clean, tidy and within easy reach with slipcovers designed to hold up to 12 books. *Plus* you can follow our recipes perfectly with a set of accurate measuring cups and spoons, as used by *The Australian Women's Weekly* Test Kitchen.

To order

Mail or fax Photocopy and complete the coupon below and post to AWW Home Library Reader Offer, ACP Direct, PO Box 7036, Sydney NSW 1028, or fax to (02) 9267 4363.

Phone Have your credit card details ready, then, if you live in Sydney, phone 9260 0000; if you live elsewhere in Australia, phone 1800 252 515 (free call, Mon-Fri, 8.30am-5.30pm).

Price

Book Holder
Australia: $13.10 (incl. GST).
Elsewhere: $A21.95.

Metric Measuring Set
Australia: $6.50 (incl. GST).
New Zealand: $A8.00.
Elsewhere: $A9.95.
Prices include postage and handling.
This offer is available in all countries.

Payment

Australian residents We accept the credit cards listed on the coupon, money orders and cheques.

Overseas residents We accept the credit cards listed on the coupon, drafts in $A drawn on an Australian bank, and also British, New Zealand and U.S. cheques in the currency of the country of issue. Credit card charges are at the exchange rate current at the time of payment.

Photocopy and complete the coupon below

☐ **Book Holder**

☐ **Metric Measuring Set**
Please indicate number(s) required.

Mr/Mrs/Ms_____

Address_____

_____

Postcode _____ Country _____

Ph: Bus. Hours:(   ) _____

I enclose my cheque/money order for $ _____
payable to ACP Direct

OR: please charge my

☐ Bankcard   ☐ Visa   ☐ MasterCard

☐ Diners Club   ☐ Amex

Card number

Expiry date ____/____

Cardholder's signature _____

Please allow up to 30 days for delivery within Australia.
Allow up to 6 weeks for overseas deliveries.
Both offers expire 31/12/02. HLAMIM01

Designer *Michele Withers*
Chief sub-editor *Julie Collard*
Sub-editor *Debbie Quick*
Test Kitchen Staff
Food editor *Pamela Clark*
Associate food editor *Karen Hammial*
Assistant food editors *Amira Ibram, Kirsty McKenzie*
Test kitchen manager *Elizabeth Hooper*
Senior home economist *Kimberley Coverdale*
Home economists *Emma Braz, Naomi Scesny, Kelly Cruickshanks, Sarah Hine, Sarah Hobbs, Alison Webb*

Home Library Staff
Editor-in-chief *Susan Tomnay*
Senior writer and editor *Georgina Bitcon*
Senior editor *Liz Neate*
Chief sub-editor *Julie Collard*
Sub-editor *Debbie Quick*
Art director *Michele Withers*
Designers *Mary Keep, Caryl Wiggins, Alison Windmill*
Studio manager *Caryl Wiggins*
Editorial coordinator *Holly van Oyen*
Book sales manager *Jennifer McDonald*
Production manager *Carol Currie*

Chief executive officer *John Alexander*
Group publisher *Jill Baker*
Publisher *Sue Wannan*

Produced by *The Australian Women's Weekly* Home Library, Sydney.
Colour separations by ACP Colour Graphics Pty Ltd, Sydney.
Printed by Dai Nippon Printing in Korea.
Published by ACP Publishing Pty Limited, 54 Park St, Sydney; GPO Box 4088, Sydney, NSW 1028.
Ph: (02) 9282 8618 Fax: (02) 9267 9438
awwhomelib@acp.com.au
www.awwbooks.com.au

AUSTRALIA: Distributed by Network Distribution Company, GPO Box 4088, Sydney, NSW 1028.
Ph: (02) 9282 8777 Fax: (02) 9264 3278.
UNITED KINGDOM: Distributed by Australian Consolidated Press (UK), Moulton Park Business Centre, Red House Rd, Moulton Park, Northampton, NN3 6AQ Ph: (01604) 497 531 Fax: (01604) 497 533 acpukltd@aol.com
CANADA: Distributed by Whitecap Books Ltd, 351 Lynn Ave, North Vancouver, BC, V7J 2C4, Ph: (604) 980 9852.
NEW ZEALAND: Distributed by Netlink Distribution Company, Level 4, 23 Hargreaves St, College Hill, Auckland 1, Ph: (9) 302 7616.
SOUTH AFRICA: Distributed by PSD Promotions (Pty) Ltd, PO Box 1175, Isando 1600, SA, Ph: (011) 392 6065,
and CNA Limited, Newsstand Division, PO Box 10799, Johannesburg 2000, SA, Ph: (011) 491 7500.

Asian meals in minutes
Includes index.
ISBN 1 86396 239 5
1. Cookery, Asian. 2. Cookery, Oriental.
(Series: Australian Women's Weekly Home Library)
641.595
© ACP Publishing Pty Limited 2001
ABN 18 053 273 546

First published 2001.